T0222519

Introducing Software Verification with Dafny Language

Proving Program Correctness

Boro Sitnikovski

Apress®

Introducing Software Verification with Dafny Language: Proving Program Correctness

Boro Sitnikovski
Skopje, North Macedonia

ISBN-13 (pbk): 978-1-4842-7977-9   ISBN-13 (electronic): 978-1-4842-7978-6
https://doi.org/10.1007/978-1-4842-7978-6

Managing Director, Apress Media LLC: Welmoed Spahr
Acquisitions Editor: Steve Anglin
Development Editor: James Markham
Coordinating Editor: Mark Powers

Cover designed by eStudioCalamar

Cover image by Eugene Golovesov on Unsplash (www.unsplash.com)

Distributed to the book trade worldwide by Apress Media, LLC, 1 New York Plaza, New York, NY 10004, U.S.A. Phone 1-800-SPRINGER, fax (201) 348-4505, e-mail orders-ny@springer-sbm.com, or visit www.springeronline.com. Apress Media, LLC is a California LLC and the sole member (owner) is Springer Science + Business Media Finance Inc (SSBM Finance Inc). SSBM Finance Inc is a **Delaware** corporation.

For information on translations, please e-mail booktranslations@springernature.com; for reprint, paperback, or audio rights, please e-mail bookpermissions@springernature.com.

Apress titles may be purchased in bulk for academic, corporate, or promotional use. eBook versions and licenses are also available for most titles. For more information, reference our Print and eBook Bulk Sales web page at http://www.apress.com/bulk-sales.

Any source code or other supplementary material referenced by the author in this book is available to readers on GitHub (github.com/apress). For more detailed information, please visit http://www.apress.com/source-code.

Printed on acid-free paper

Gladly dedicated to my family, especially to the love
Of my life, my wife Dijana, together with
my daughter Zhaklina and my son Hristijan.

Table of Contents

About the Author

Boro Sitnikovski has over 10 years of experience working professionally as a software engineer. He started programming using the Assembly programming language on an Intel x86 at the age of 10. While in high school, he won several prizes in competitive programming, ranging from fourth to third and first places.

He is an informatics graduate; his bachelor's thesis was titled "Programming in Haskell Using Algebraic Data Structures," and his master's thesis was titled "Formal Verification of Instruction Sets in Virtual Machines." He has also published papers on software verification. His other research interests include programming languages, mathematics, logic, algorithms, and writing correct software.

He is a strong believer in the open source philosophy and contributes to various open source projects.

In his spare time, he enjoys time with his family.

About the Technical Reviewer

Aleksandar Stankov has over 10 years of experience working professionally as a software engineer, software architect, and CTO. He has worked on different projects in the United States, Norway, Germany, and Macedonia. He is a computer engineer with a bachelor's in brain–computer interface and a master's in project management where his thesis was titled "Quality management in software projects."

Last year, he was focused on founding a startup for mental health, called "Relaxifyapp," that would improve the well-being of people using the mobile app.

His interests include blockchain, microservices, Web 3.0, and mobile apps.

Preface

I was always interested in understanding things from first principles. I believe this interest naturally led to learning mathematics. Writing is a way for me to clarify my thoughts,[1] which resulted in the book you're reading at the moment.

Every programmer in their career will run into bugs caused by themselves, their logic, and reasoning. After the first few bug fixes, it becomes a rather irritating experience. A programmer will do their best to avoid introducing bugs in software. However, it's not just a matter of ego or avoiding being irritated. Depending on the criticality, some software systems must be designed in such a way where failure is not an option.

Various tools exist to address this, both software applications and theoretical concepts. In this book, we will cover some of them, including algorithms (computation), the English language (and its vagueness), and the mathematical language (and its preciseness, compared to the English language).

The English language is also important – we will describe the concepts in this book using it. This language can be a little bit vague, though; thus, we will circle back to the first principles (mathematics) and see how we can be as precise as possible.

We need a framework in order to be able to express mathematical concepts.[2] Dafny is one tool (programming language) that will allow us to

---

[1] "Writing is nature's way of letting you know how sloppy your thinking is."
—Dick Guindon

[2] "Often people talk about mathematics being useful for programming. It works both ways. Programming (esp. functional programming) has deepened my understanding of mathematics in numerous ways." —Dan Piponi

research these and is what we will use throughout the book. It is not the *only* tool though, and the concepts that we will introduce in this book will be easily applicable to other languages that allow for software verification.

There are several platforms for software verification. Formal verification is based on mathematical proofs, and the software platforms are categorized into manual provers and automatic provers. Among the manual ones, some of the most popular are the programming languages Coq [12] (based on type theory), Idris [14], etc. Automated theorem provers use algorithms to automatically deduce a given theorem, and Dafny belongs to this family.

There are already good writings on Dafny, but the purpose of this book is to be self-contained and not assume a lot of background besides basic programming skills. Knowing how to program is not a strict necessity, although it may help in grasping some concepts. The book also assumes some basic experience with mathematics, such as functions and elementary algebra.

To get the most of it, the recommended approach for the book is to follow along and write the code as it's being explained instead of reading passively.

Thanks to my family, coworkers, and friends for the support, and thank you for purchasing this book! I tried to introduce concepts as clearly as I could, and I added examples and exercises, which I believe are crucial to understanding. I hope that you will learn new techniques from this book. Have fun!

Languages and Systems

In this chapter, we will cover the most foundational theoretical concepts (starting from first principles) that will be necessary for our journey to prove software correctness.

A lot of my programmer friends get scared away whenever they hear the word "mathematics." Unfortunately, there's no getting around it, and in this chapter, we'll see why. However, we will try to be as descriptive as possible, and English will be our friend, so stay a while and read!

Languages provide us a way to transfer some message or information to someone, or even save some piece of information for our future self, by writing it down; humans tend to forget easily. There are a lot of different languages, but that's the essence of them all – transferring information.

Now, to talk about its structure, a language consists of a finite set of symbols (A, B, C, ...) and a way to combine those so that strings (list of symbols) can be formed: ABBA, CAB, etc. In addition, it consists of grammar that tells us how to form valid strings. For example, in the English language, "Hi, how are you?" is a valid statement, whereas "hi, how" isn't.[1]

A language affects how a person thinks, as different languages consist of different grammars. For example, to pronounce the number 23 in English, we say "twenty-three." However, for example, in Slovenian, we say "three twenty." This is because the rule to construct numbers is different between these two languages. Thus, knowing different languages enriches not only our vocabulary but also the different rules possible to construct statements.

---

[1] The definition of validity varies in different contexts. In this context, we say that a statement is valid if it makes sense and allows for communication between parties. For example, if someone said to you "hi, how," there is a very small chance of having a useful dialog.

But why care about different rules? Well, some languages are good for some things and not as good for other things; there is no "best" language. Similarly, in programming, it may be easier for some problems to be solved in C (one programming language) than in Haskell (another programming language).

This book is written using the English language; however, this language has its limitations (as every other language). To see one limitation, note that in computing, we usually talk about algorithms and numbers, which are simply logical expressions. Now, consider the statement "There exists a number such that it's greater than two and there exists a number such that it's greater than three." There's some vagueness involved here. First, is the first number the same as the other one, or must they be different? Second, are we talking about positive numbers only, or are negative also allowed? And so on.

It'd be good if we had a framework (language) to express our ideas as precisely as possible, but also keeping the essence and removing all other redundant distractions, for example, unnecessary words such as "such that" in "there exists a number n such that it's positive."

It's okay to be informal (that's why we use English), but sometimes, formality is needed, especially when we are to represent our ideas as computer programs since computers will do *exactly* what we tell them to.

If languages allow us to transfer some message, then **formal systems** (using some language) allow us to transfer some abstract idea. Formal systems lie at the heart of mathematics, and through them, the foundations are specified.

Before we can construct a proof of software correctness, we need to understand what proof is and what it means for a piece of proof to be valid. The purpose of formal systems is to enable reasoning for logical proof in terms of their *form*, rather than their *content*. This level of abstraction makes formal systems powerful tools.

ⓘ **Definition 1** A **formal system** is a model of abstract reasoning that consists of

- A *formal language* containing

  - A finite set of *symbols*, which can be combined into finite strings called *formulas*

  - *Grammar*, which is a set of rules that represent well-formed formulas

- A set of *axioms* – formulas accepted as valid without proof

- A set of *inference rules* that allow the construction of new, valid formulas based on existing ones, called theorems

---

Within a given formal system, the grammar determines which formulas are *syntactically* valid, while inference rules determine which formulas are *semantically* valid. The symbols as such have no special meaning, while the inference rules define the meaning. The difference between these two is very important. For example, taking the English language as a (very complicated) formal system, the sentence "Colorless green ideas sleep furiously" is syntactically valid because different types of words are used in the appropriate places, but it is semantically meaningless.

Once a formal system is defined, other formal systems can extend it. For example, set theory is based on first-order logic, which itself is based on propositional logic, which is a formal system. These theories will be discussed later.

In the following example, we will consider the "MU" problem as a formal system, represented as follows:

1. Formal language

    1. The set of symbols is {M, I, U}.

    2. A given string is well-formed if the first letter is M and there are no other M letters. Example: M, MIUIU, MUUUIII.

2. MI is the initial string, axiom.

3. The inference rules are defined as in Table 1.

Table 1. *Example inference rules*

No	Rule	Description	Example
1	xI → xIU	Apply U to a string that ends in I	MI turns MIU
2	Mx → Mxx	Double the string after M	MIU turns MIUIU
3	xIIIy → xUy	Replace III with U in a string	MUIIIU turns MUUU
4	xUUy → xy	Remove UU from a string	MUUU turns MU

In the inference rules, the symbols M, I, and U are part of the system, while x and y are variables that represent any list of symbols (string). For example, rule number 2 can be applied to MI, where x = I, but rule number 1 for x = M can also be applied. Thus, from MI, one can derive MII but can also derive MIU, respectively. Another example is MII to which rule number 2 for x = II and rule number 1 for x = MI can be applied.

The following example shows how to get from MI to MIIU:

1. MI (axiom)

2. MII (rule 2, x = I)

3. MIIII (rule 2, x = II)

4. MIIIIIIII (rule 2, x = IIII)

5. MUIIIII (rule 3, x = M, y = IIIII)

6. MUUII (rule 3, x = MU, y = II)

7. MII (rule 4, x = M, y = II)

8. MIIU (rule 1, x = MI)

Now, consider the following puzzle: Can we derive MU, starting from MI in this system? To prove whether this is possible or not, an invariant will be used together with mathematical induction (these two terms will be discussed in more detail later). One way to get to MU is by using rule number 3, and to be able to apply it, the number of consecutive Is in a string must be divisible by 3. The invariant is represented as follows: in a given string, there is no consecutive Is whose length is divisible by 3. The proof (by cases) follows:

1. There is one I for the initial axiom. The invariant passes (one is not divisible by 3).

2. Applying rule 2 will double the number of I, so it can be I, II, IIII, IIIIIII (generally, 2^n times I). The invariant passes (2^n is not divisible by 3, for any n).

3. Applying rule 3 will reduce the number of I by 3, but $2^n - 3$ is not divisible by 3. The invariant passes.

We've shown that with the starting axiom MI, it is not possible to get to MU. But if we look carefully, we've used a different formal system to reason about MU (i.e., divisibility by 3, which is not part of the MU system itself).

This is because the puzzle cannot be solved in its own system. Otherwise, if we wanted to solve it in its own system using some algorithm, this algorithm would keep trying different inference rules of MU indefinitely (not knowing that MU is impossible).

In any formal system, there are infinitely many levels of expression: object level, meta-level, meta-meta-level, and so on. Meta-levels include expressions of the system outside the system itself, unrestricted by the system's rules. The object level is more limited, where the expressions that are included are only using the rules of the system itself. For example, for the MU system, we had to exit the system (meta) to solve a given problem in the system (object).

The reason for this distinction of levels (object and meta-level) can be explained as follows. Assuming that in a given system, a value of A can be replaced with B, the rule "A can be replaced with B" is at the meta-level (i.e., in English, instead of the language of the formal system). That meta-sentence can be formalized in the system itself, but there are infinite meta-levels for formalization, so not all of them can be formalized.

Thus, sometimes, it is better to reason about a formal system outside of the system (at different meta-levels) since the object level of the system can be limiting; as the famous saying goes, "to think outside the box." It is useful to have experience with different formal systems and to combine them as needed.

With the help of the English language so far, we are slowly entering the realm of mathematics. Mathematics is all about using different formal systems; like playing a game according to some specific rules.

One of the most popular categories of formal systems is logic, an attempt to capture human reasoning represented with symbols. In the following chapters, we'll be looking at different logical systems.

CHAPTER 1

Our First Program

Dafny is an imperative programming language that allows software to be verified through preconditions, postconditions, and invariants. Designed by Rustan Leino and developed by Microsoft since 2009, Dafny is used in academia and the industry and is regularly used in software verification competitions.

As a programming language, Dafny shares many features with languages from the "imperative" family or paradigm, such as C, C++, and Java. There are functions and procedures (methods), variables, types, loops, conditional expressions, arrays, numbers, etc. However, it also shares concepts with languages from the "functional" family, such as algebraic data structures, pattern matching, and recursion.

Besides these concepts, Dafny can also serve as an automated theorem prover. However, this automation is not perfect – sometimes, it is necessary to assist it to be able to prove a certain theorem. For example, Dafny does not always know that a certain loop is terminating, so we need to hint at it that it actually does. We'll cover this in detail in the later chapters.

In this chapter, we will show how to configure and install the Dafny programming language on your machine. For that purpose, we will be using VS Code (Visual Studio Code) – an editor that allows us to write code and run programs. It is not the only editor that supports Dafny, but we found this one to be particularly easy to install and use.

© Boro Sitnikovski 2022
B. Sitnikovski, *Introducing Software Verification with Dafny Language*,
https://doi.org/10.1007/978-1-4842-7978-6_1

You can download and install VS Code using the official webpage https://code.visualstudio.com, choosing the correct platform for your computer. If everything went well, you should see the same as Figure 1-1.

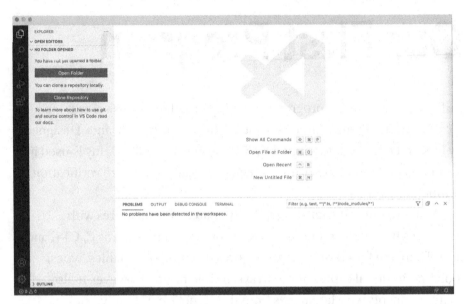

Figure 1-1. *VS Code first screen*

Next, to install Dafny, navigate to the menu "View ➤ Command Palette" and select "Install Extensions." Search for "Dafny" and choose to install it.

After you installed it, make sure to restart the VS Code application. When you start it again, the installation will proceed.

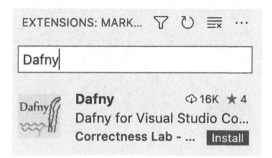

Figure 1-2. *Dafny extension*

Note that Dafny requires .NET core runtime; if you don't have it installed on your system, it will prompt you to install it first.

Once Dafny is installed, we can start working our way toward our first program. To do that, create a file named "test.dfy", save it anywhere, and drop the following contents in it:

```
1  method Main() {
2    print "Hello, World!\n";
3  }
```

If, once you open it with VS Code and when you press F5, you get the same as in Figure 1-3, then congratulations! We just ran our first program.

Users > boro > Desktop > ≡ test.dfy

```
1    method Main() {
2    |   print "Hello, World!\n";
3    }
```

| PROBLEMS | OUTPUT | DEBUG CONSOLE | TERMINAL | bash + v [] 🗑 ^ × |

```
"/usr/local/bin/dotnet" "/Users/boro/.vscode/extensions/correctnesslab.dafny-vscode-1.
6.0/out/resources/dafny/Dafny.dll" "/Users/boro/Desktop/test.dfy" /verifyAllModules /c
ompile:3 /spillTargetCode:1 /out:bin/test
boro@bor0:~$ "/usr/local/bin/dotnet" "/Users/boro/.vscode/extensions/correctnesslab.da
fny-vscode-1.6.0/out/resources/dafny/Dafny.dll" "/Users/boro/Desktop/test.dfy" /verify
AllModules /compile:3 /spillTargetCode:1 /out:bin/test

Dafny program verifier finished with 0 verified, 0 errors
Wrote textual form of target program to test.cs
Running...

Hello, World!
boro@bor0:~$ ▌
```

Figure 1-3. *First program*

The example code defines a method called Main and then uses the
`print` statement to print something to the screen. Dafny will automatically
execute (at runtime) all the code in the method named Main, similarly as
other programming languages do.

But "Hello World" programs are boring, right? Let's slightly modify our
example to see the full power of Dafny:

```
1   method Main()
2     ensures 3 * 2 == 6
3   {
4     print "Hello, World!\n";
5   }
```

We added the statement ensures 3 * 2 == 6 between the declaration of Main and its body; this part is called the **specifications** area. If we press F5 again, Dafny happily runs the program; that is, Dafny proved that $3 \cdot 2 = 6$.

However, let's now try the following:

```
1  method Main()
2    ensures 3 * 2 == 7
3  {
4    print "Hello, World!\n";
5  }
```

If we try to run this program, Dafny will complain (at compile time) with the following error:

```
1  /Users/boro/Desktop/test.dfy(3,0): Error: A postcondition
   might not hold on this return path.
```

It is as if Dafny somehow has knowledge about mathematics built-in!

There is an important distinction to be made here between compile time and runtime. If a program compiles successfully, that is, Dafny manages to prove whatever we ask from it, then it will proceed to execute the code at runtime. The print statement occurred at runtime, while the ensures statement occurred at compile time.

We have already covered formal systems. With this example, we can see how Dafny incorporates *at least* two formal systems:

1. Mathematical logic (at the compile time level)

2. Evaluation of programs (at the runtime level)

We will cover these in depth in the upcoming chapters.

✎ Exercise 1   What will Dafny return for the following program? What if we change 4 to 3? Subsequently, what if we change `Example` to `Main`?

```
1  method Example()
2    ensures 1 + 2 == 4
3  {
4    print "Hello, World!\n";
5  }
```

CHAPTER 2

Logic

In this chapter, we will cover two of the most important branches of mathematical logic.

2.1. Propositional Logic

We've seen a very brief example of how Dafny incorporates some sort of logic within it. In this section, we'll cover logic in more detail.

The most basic level of logic is propositional logic that deals with the study of **statements**, sentences that are either true ($\top$) or false ($\bot$). More specifically, here's the description of these statements (formulas):

1. The logical constants $\top$ and $\bot$ and the expression letters (variables) a, b, ... are formulas.

2. If a and b are formulas, then $a \wedge b$ (and), $a \vee b$ (or), $\neg a$ (negation), $a \rightarrow b$ (implication), and $a \leftrightarrow b$ (equivalence) are also formulas.

For example, we could say a: "Salad is organic food", and thus, a is a true statement. Another one is a: "Stone is organic food", and thus, a is a false statement. The sentence "Hello!" is neither true nor false, so it is not a statement.

© Boro Sitnikovski 2022
B. Sitnikovski, *Introducing Software Verification with Dafny Language*,
https://doi.org/10.1007/978-1-4842-7978-6_2

 Definition 1   The statement $a \wedge b$ (*conjunction*) is true when *both* a and b are true.

For example, the statement "I love milk and sugar" is true only if "I love milk" and "I love sugar" are both true.

***Table 2-1.** Logical "and"*

a	b	a ∧ b
⊤	⊤	⊤
⊤	⊥	⊥
⊥	⊤	⊥
⊥	⊥	⊥

In Dafny, we can represent it using the following code:

```
1  method Conjunction ()
2    ensures 1 + 2 == 3 && 1 * 2 == 2
3  {}
```

Note how the body is empty, meaning that Dafny will do nothing at runtime; we're just asking it to evaluate the logical expression at compile time.

 Definition 2   The statement $a \vee b$ (disjunction) is true when *at least one* of a or b is true.

For example, the statement "I want milk or sugar" is true only if at least one of the statements "I want milk" and "I want sugar" is also true. This is also known as the inclusive "or."

This definition of "or" might be a bit counterintuitive to the way we use it in day-to-day speaking. When we say "I like milk or sugar," we normally mean one of them but not both. This is known as exclusive "or."

***Table 2-2.** Logical "or"*

a	b	a ∨ b
T	T	T
T	⊥	T
⊥	T	T
⊥	⊥	⊥

In Dafny, we can represent it using the following code:

```
1  method Disjunction()
2     ensures 1 + 2 == 3 || 1 * 2 == 3
3  {}
```

Note that Dafny will not return an error, as true || false is true.

  Definition 3   The **negation** of the statement a is the statement $\neg a$ that has the opposite truth of a.

The negation connective simply swaps the truthiness of a statement. The easiest way to negate any statement is to just prepend "It is not the case that ..." to it. For example, the negation of "I like milk" is "It is not the case that I like milk," or simply "I don't like milk."

Table 2-3. *Logical negation*

a	¬*a*
⊤	⊥
⊥	⊤

In Dafny, we can represent it using the following code:

```
1  method Negation()
2    ensures ! (1 * 2 == 3)
3  {}
```

---

i   **Definition 4**   The **Implication** of the statements *a* and *b* is defined as the statement "If *a* then *b*", or with symbols $a \rightarrow b$. It represents a true value whenever *a* is true, *b* is also true.

Table 2-4. *Logical implication*

a	b	a → b
⊤	⊤	⊤
⊤	⊥	⊥
⊥	⊤	⊤
⊥	⊥	⊤

Another way to understand implication is in terms of *obligation*; $a \rightarrow b$ is a promise that if *a* happens, then *b* also happens. For example, for *a*: "Today is your birthday" and *b*: "I brought a cake", it follows that $a \rightarrow b$ represents the promise "If today is your birthday, then I brought a cake".

Further, there are four different cases to consider for this implication's value:

1. "Today is your birthday and I brought a cake." The promise is kept, so the implication is true.

2. "Today is your birthday, but I did not bring a cake." The promise is not kept, so the implication is untrue.

3. "Today is not your birthday, and I brought a cake." Is the promise kept? Better question: Has the promise been broken? The condition the promise is based on, that is, the statement "today is your birthday", is not satisfied, so we say that the promise is not broken. The implication is true.

4. "Today is not your birthday and I did not bring a cake." Again, the obligation condition is not satisfied, so the obligation is not violated. The implication is true.

This definition of implication might be a bit counterintuitive to the way we use it in day-to-day speaking. When we say "If it rains, then the ground is wet," we usually mean both that "If the ground is wet, then it rains" and "If it rains, then the ground is wet." This is known as logical equivalence and is denoted as $a \leftrightarrow b$, or simply a iff b.

In Dafny, implications can be represented as follows:

```
1  method Imp1()
2    ensures 1 + 2 == 3 ==> 2 + 2 == 4
3  {}
4
5  method Imp2() // Dafny can't prove this, as expected
6    ensures 1 + 2 == 3 ==> 2 + 2 == 5
```

```
 7  {}
 8  method Imp3()
 9     ensures 1 + 2 == 4 ==> 2 + 2 == 4
10  {}
11
12  method Imp4()
13     ensures 1 + 2 == 4 ==> 2 + 2 == 5
14  {}
```

> **ⓘ** **Definition 5**   The **equivalence** of the statements a and b is
> the statement "a if and only if b". The statement $a \leftrightarrow b$ is true
> whenever a and b have the same truth.

Table 2-5. *Logical equivalence*

a	b	$a \leftrightarrow b$
T	T	T
T	⊥	⊥
⊥	T	⊥
⊥	⊥	T

In Dafny, equivalences can be represented as follows:

```
1  method Equiv1()
2     ensures 1 + 1 == 2 <==> 2 + 2 == 4
3  {}
4
5  method Equiv2() // Dafny can't prove this, as expected
6     ensures 1 + 1 == 2 <==> 2 + 2 == 5
```

```
 7  {}
 8
 9  method Equiv3() // Dafny can't prove this, as expected
10     ensures 1 + 1 == 3 <==> 2 + 2 == 4
11  {}
12
13  method Equiv4()
14     ensures 1 + 1 == 3 <==> 2 + 2 == 5
15  {}
```

 Exercise 1   What will Dafny return for the following program? What if we change 5 to 3?

```
1  method Conj()
2     ensures 1 + 2 == 5 && 2 + 2 == 4
3  {}
```

 Exercise 2   What will Dafny return for the following program? Does changing 5 to 3 have any effect on the result?

```
1  method Disj()
2     ensures 1 + 2 == 5 || 2 + 2 == 4
3  {}
```

 Exercise 3   What will Dafny return for the following program? What if we change 2 to 3?

```
1  method NotEqual()
2     ensures !(1 + 1 == 2)
3  {}
```

 Exercise 4   What will Dafny return for the following

program? What if we change 4 to 3? Subsequently, what if we change 5 to 6?

```
1  method Impl()
2     ensures 1 + 2 == 4 ==> 2 + 5 == 7
3  {}
```

2.2. Predicate Logic and Quantifiers

In this section, we will extend propositional logic with a few concepts, therefore making it more powerful.

ⓘ **Definition 6**   A **predicate** is a sentence that contains one or

more variables and which becomes an expression by concretizing (assigning) a value to each of the variables from a set of values.

We denote predicates using capital letters and in parentheses the variables on which they depend (arguments). For example, $P(x)$, $Q(x, y, z)$. Predicate logic (first-order logic) extends propositional logic with **predicates** and **quantifiers**:

1. The predicate $P(x)$ receives as input x and outputs either true ($\top$) or false ($\bot$).

2. Two quantifiers: $\forall$ (universal quantifier) and $\exists$ (existential quantifier).

An example of a predicate is $P(x)$: "x is organic food", where $P(\text{salad}) = \top$, but $P(\text{stone}) = \bot$, since stone is not an organic food.

The universal quantifier indicates that the predicate will be true for **all** possible inputs for x: $\forall x, P(x)$. Alternatively, the existential quantifier indicates that the predicate will be true for **at least one** input for x: $\exists x, P(x)$.

One example of combining a predicate with a universal quantifier is $P(x)$: "x is a mammal". Then $\forall x, P(x)$ is true for all x in the set of people. For another example, we can set $P(x)$: "x knows math" and $\exists x, P(x)$ to express that there is at least one person who knows math.

The negation of these quantifiers is defined as follows:

1. $\neg (\forall x, P(x)) \leftrightarrow \exists x, \neg P(x)$

2. $\neg(\exists x, P(x)) \leftrightarrow \forall x, \neg P(x)$

In first-order logic, predicates act as functions that take an input and produce an output. The predicate cannot be true or false until a certain value is applied. However, the quantifiers $\forall$ and $\exists$ "close" a predicate by determining truthiness, not requiring a value to be applied.

A **meta-predicate** can be defined that acts as a function on predicates. For example, we can let $\Gamma(P)$ define the statement "there exists a person x such that $P(x)$ is true". The truthiness of $\Gamma(P)$ cannot be determined until a *specific predicate P* is entered. But it can be quantified through P by constructing a sentence, for example, $\forall P, \Gamma(P)$. In English, this sentence translates to "For any predicate (property) P, there is a person who satisfies that predicate." These meta-predicates belong to *second-order logic* because they quantify over first-order predicates. Predicates of third, fourth, and nth orders can be defined similarly.

Thus, **higher-order logics** extend quantifiers[1] to predicates. For example, second-order logic quantifies over sets. Third-order logic quantifies over sets of sets (families) and so on. This "vertical" climbing in the hierarchy of logical systems brings power, but at a price.

Propositional logic (zero order) is completely decisive.[2] Predicate logic (first order) is not decisive, and from Gödel's theorems of incompleteness,[3] one must choose one of completeness and consistency. But at least there is still an algorithm that can determine whether a given piece of proof is valid or not. For second (or higher) order logic, this property is also lost – one must choose between completeness, consistency, and an algorithm for detecting proof.

In practice, second-order predicates are not used as often, and higher-order predicates are almost unnecessary. To show an example of a second-order predicate, we consider the axioms of the mathematician Giuseppe Peano (1858–1932) for natural numbers.

---

[1] Since unlimited quantification leads to inconsistency, type theory is an attempt to avoid it.

[2] This means that there is a decision algorithm that, for any expression, will always return a correct value (true or false), instead of running indefinitely or producing an incorrect value.

[3] Refer to Appendix A for more details.

Definition 7   Peano's axioms are a formalization of natural numbers.

There are a total of nine axioms, but we will list only a few:

- $0 \in \mathbb{N}$, that is, 0 is a natural number.

- $\forall x \in \mathbb{N}$, $S(x) \in \mathbb{N}$, that is, for every natural number x, it holds that $S(x)$ is a natural number (successor function).

- $\forall x \in \mathbb{N}$, $x = x$, that is, for every natural number x, $x = x$ (equality is reflexive).

The ninth axiom is the induction axiom which we will cover in detail in Chapter 7.

All of the axioms are expressions in first-order logic. An exception to this is the induction axiom, which is represented in second order because it quantifies on predicates. These basic axioms can be further extended with arithmetic operations such as sum and multiplication.

Here is an example proof of the reflexivity of natural numbers:

```
1  method NatReflexivity()
2    ensures forall n : nat :: n == n
3  {}
```

The forall keyword introduces quantification, and the n : nat part tells that n is a natural number (of type nat).

If you try to run the example, you might notice that it produces a warning about "triggers." Feel free to ignore those, as we will cover them in detail later when we'll talk about predicates.

Exercise 5   What will Dafny return for the following program?

```
1  method WeirdNatReflexivity()
2    ensures forall n : nat :: n == n + 1
3  {}
```

 Exercise 6   What will Dafny return for the following program?

```
1  method NotThatWeirdNatReflexivity()
2    ensures forall n : nat :: !(n == n + 1)
3  {}
```

 Exercise 7   What will Dafny return for the following program?

```
1  method NatEleven()
2    ensures exists n : nat :: n == 11
3  {}
```

 Exercise 8   What does the following program prove?

```
1  method InterestingFact(n : nat)
2    ensures forall x :: x + 1 == 2 <==> x == 1
3  {}
```

CHAPTER 3

Computation

So far, we covered basic functionalities in Dafny that deal with mathematical logic. In this chapter, we will introduce more useful concepts with Dafny.

 Definition 1 An **algorithm (procedure)** represents a sequence of steps in some process. At the lowest level, a procedure represents operations upon symbols in a formal system, e.g. substitution, comparison, duplication. On a higher level, a procedure may represent a sequence of arithmetical operations, e.g. within Peano axioms.

That definition might sound a bit too abstract, so let's take a look at an example algorithm of frying an egg. It consists of the following steps, roughly:

1. Open the fridge

2. Take an egg

3. Close the fridge

4. Break the egg

5. Spill it into a frying pan

6. Start frying it

© Boro Sitnikovski 2022
B. Sitnikovski, *Introducing Software Verification with Dafny Language*,
https://doi.org/10.1007/978-1-4842-7978-6_3

Now, all of these steps together describe the process of frying an egg. However, we can notice that the step "Start frying it" is rather abstract. What does it mean to fry it? Or, for another, what does it mean to open the fridge? Do we do it with a hand? Does the fridge have a handle at all? There are different answers to these questions, depending on the abstraction level we're working. In everyday communication, it's okay to be a bit vague, whereas when working with a programming language, all of these specifics must be addressed.

Computation is a type of formal system; the symbols being ones and zeroes, and the inference rules representing procedures. It comes in many forms: for proofs, and e.g. in Prolog, deduction is a form of computation; for algebra, it is the simplification of expressions; in Lisp, it is the operations upon symbols; in Haskell, computation at the type level corresponds to proofs, while computation at the value level corresponds to recursive functions.

3.1. Variables and Assertions

Variables can be declared using the keyword var, and they can be used to store any values. We can also test **assertions** against them:

```
1  method Main()
2  {
3    var v := 3;
4    assert 0 <= v;
5  }
```

In this case, the assertion claims that the value of v will be positive and Dafny confirms that. In general, assertions allow us to check some logical facts about the behavior of our code.

However, if we try to prove something false, for example:

```
1  method Main()
2  {
3    var v := 3;
4    assert 0 > v;
5  }
```

in this case, Dafny will return an error:

```
1  test.dfy(4,12): Error: assertion violation
2  Execution trace:
3      (0,0): anon0
4
5  Dafny program verifier finished with 1 verified, 1 error
```

In addition, we can also specify the type of variable. However, this is optional in most cases, as Dafny can automatically infer it.

```
1  method Main()
2  {
3    var v2 : nat := 3;
4    var v1 : int := -3;
5  }
```

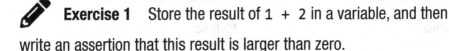 **Exercise 1**   Store the result of 1 + 2 in a variable, and then write an assertion that this result is larger than zero.

3.2. Methods and Functions

We already used **methods**. They are similar to procedures in your favorite programming language, and they can be defined as follows:

```
1  method Abs(x : int) returns (y : int)
2  {
3    ...
4  }
```

The preceding code indicates that Abs is a method that receives x of type int (i.e., integer) and returns some y (also integer). So if we tried to call this method with a different type other than int, Dafny would return an error – types allow us to add constraints (more structure) to our code.

Besides methods, we can also define **functions**. A function named AbsFun that receives a number and returns a number can be defined as follows:

```
1  function AbsFun(x : int) : int
2  {
3    if x < 0 then -x else x
4  }
```

The distinction between a function and a method can be a bit confusing. We list the differences in Table 3-1.

Table 3-1. *Difference between a function and a method*

Function	Method
Contains a single expression	Can contain multiple expressions
Can be used in the specification section	Cannot be used in the specification section
Cannot be used within the body of a method	Can be used within the body of a method
Not part of the final program (acts as a substitution at the compile level)	Part of the final program (acts as a computation at the runtime level)

With AbsFun, we've seen the syntax of if-then-else: if <conditional> then <command1> else <command2>. Unlike functions, which can only contain a single expression, we can also use conditionals within a method in a form where it can contain multiple expressions.

We now show the full definition of the method Abs:

```
1   method Abs(x : int) returns (y : int)
2   {
3     if x < 0
4     {
5       // some expression...
6       return -x;
7     }
8     else
9     {
10      // some other expression...
11      return x;
12    }
13  }
```

Even though Abs and AbsFun represent different computations at different execution levels, both of them correspond to the same mathematical definition:

$$Abs(x) = \begin{cases} -x & x < 0, \\ x & \text{otherwise} \end{cases}$$

There is also a way to tell Dafny to compile functions, rather than just substituting when compiling. Doing this allows us to use function calls within methods. We can define them using the function method declaration:

```
1   function method AbsFun2(x : int) : int
2   {
3     if x < 0 then -x else x
4   }
```

Having it defined this way, we can print its computed value:

```
1  method Main()
2  {
3    var x := AbsFun2(123); // This works fine (function method)
4    print(x);
5    //x := AbsFun(123); // This will produce an error (function)
6    x := Abs(123); // This works fine (method)
7    print(x);
8  }
```

With the syntax [: (T1,T2...) -> T] := (x1,x2...) => expr, function methods can also be defined inline, where the type is optionally specified:

```
1  method Main()
2  {
3    var CoolAbs : int -> int := (x) => if x < 0 then -x
     else x;
4    var x := CoolAbs(123);
5    print(x);
6  }
```

Finally, methods can receive and return more than one argument:

```
1  method MultipleReturns(x : int, y : int) returns (more :
       int, less : int)
2  {
3    more := x + y;
4    less := x - y;
5  }
```

The method MultipleReturns will accept two arguments, x and y, and return two arguments: the first returned argument will be the sum of x and y, and the second one will be the difference of x and y.

Exercise 2   Implement a method that calculates and returns the product of two numbers.

 Exercise 3   Implement a function that calculates and returns the product of two numbers. How does the implementation differ from the previous exercise?

3.3. Predicates (Triggers) and Lemmas

Besides procedures and functions, we can also define **predicates**. A predicate is simply a function that returns a bool (true or false):

```
1  predicate Reflexivity(n: nat)
2  {
3    n == n
4  }
```

Reflexivity will return either true or false. We can now use it in a method as follows:

```
1  method NatReflexivity(n : nat)
2    ensures forall n : nat :: Reflexivity(n)
3  {}
```

This method corresponds to NatReflexivity in Chapter 2, but in this case, it does not produce a warning about triggers. Triggers tell Dafny when to instantiate a quantified formula – they are an internal mechanism that executes when we use quantifiers, and separating the logical expressions into predicates satisfies the triggers mechanism.

In the example, Dafny will notify us with the message "Selected triggers: {Reflexivity(n)}"; this is not a warning or an error, it's a diagnostic message that provides more details about the triggers. It can be safely ignored.

Dafny also supports defining so-called **lemmas**. In the context of mathematics, a lemma is the same as a more minor theorem (a mathematical fact such as $1 + 1 = 2$), where it's more common for lemmas to be applied within theorems, even though applying theorems within theorems is also possible. In the context of Dafny, a lemma is pretty similar to a method with the additional constraint of it being a ghost – meaning the method will not be available to be used at runtime; we just want to check its properties during compile time.

Here's one way to define a lemma:

```
1  lemma NatReflexivityLemma(n : nat)
2    ensures forall n : nat :: Reflexivity(n)
3  {}
```

Exercise 4   Implement a predicate that is satisfied when a number greater than zero is passed to it and then use this predicate in a method.

3.4. Loops

A **loop** represents one of the most basic characteristics of computation; it repeats a piece of code until a specific condition is satisfied. One way loops can be represented is through recursive functions. Recursive functions can represent any kind of computation.

Definition 2   Recursive functions are functions that refer to themselves. These functions contain

- A simple base case (or cases) – a terminating case that returns a value

- A set of rules that reduce the other cases toward the base case(s)

One such example of recursion is the Power function, defined as follows:

$$\text{Power}(x, n) = \begin{cases} 1, & \text{if } n = 0, \\ x \cdot \text{Power}(x, n-1), & \text{otherwise} \end{cases}$$

For example, Power(3, 2) = 3 · Power(3, 1), then Power(3, 1) = 3 · Power(3, 0), and Power(3, 0) = 1. It follows that Power(3, 2) = 9. Even though this function references itself, the cases reduce the expressions to the base case, so it eventually terminates.

That is, Power really just represents x^n, or $\prod_{i=1}^{n} x$. We can represent this function in Dafny as follows:

```
1  function Power(x : nat, n : nat) : nat
2  {
3    if n == 0 then 1 else x * Power(x, n-1)
4  }
```

Dafny will produce a warning for that definition because it doesn't know that Power really terminates. We can fix that by adding decreases n between the function definition and the function body:

```
1  function Power(x : nat, n : nat) : nat
2    decreases n
3  {
4    if n == 0 then 1 else x * Power(x, n-1)
5  }
```

We will talk more about termination later.

We can represent the same method in a tail-recursive[1] way:

```
1  function PowerTail(x : nat, n : nat, p : nat) : nat
2    decreases n
3  {
4    if n == 0 then p else PowerTail(x, n-1, x*p)
5  }
```

Power and PowerTail express the same computation, differently. Consider the computation of 2^5:

```
1  Power(2, 5) = 2 * Power(2, 4) = 2 * 2 * Power(2, 3) = 2 * 2
        * 2 * Power(2, 2) = 2 * 2 * 2 * 2 * Power(2, 1) = 2 * 2
        * 2 * 2 * 2 * Power(2, 0) = 2 * 2 * 2 * 2 * 2 * 1 = 32
2  PowerTail(2, 5, 1) = PowerTail(2, 4, 2) = PowerTail(2,
        3, 4) = PowerTail(2, 2, 8) = PowerTail(2, 1, 16) =
        PowerTail(2, 0, 32) = 32
```

We can test these two functions as follows:

```
1  method Example()
2    ensures PowerTail(2, 5) == 32
3    ensures PowerTail(2, 5, 1) == 32
4  {}
```

---

[1] Tail recursion represents a process where the value to be returned, at any point in computation, is captured completely by its arguments.

Further, we can represent the same algorithm as a method using the well-known keyword while:

```
1   method PowerMethod(x : nat, n : nat) returns (p : nat)
2   {
3     p := 1;
4     var i := n;
5
6     while i != 0
7     {
8       p := p * x;
9       i := i - 1;
10    }
11  }
```

In this method, a variable i is created with an initial value of n. As long as i is not 0, we keep multiplying by x, that is, x*x*...*x, for n times.

Defining algorithms this way is more explicit and thus more complex – it is not immediately obvious which algorithm is defined by just looking at the code.

As before, we need to add decreases between lines 6 and 7.

Dafny can represent both *primitive recursive* (bounded loops) and *(general) recursive* functions (unbounded loops), as long as we prove they terminate.

As we saw, there are two ways to represent loops: as a function and as a method. We will later prove that Power and PowerMethod are logically equivalent.

Exercise 5   Evaluate `Power(5, 3)` using pen and paper.

 Exercise 6   Write a function `Summation` that accepts a natural number n and returns the sum from 0 to n, that is, 0 + 1 + ... + n.

 Exercise 7   Write a function `Summation2` that accepts natural numbers n, and another one s that represents the current calculated sum, and returns the sum from 0 to n, that is, 0 + 1 + ... + n (tail recursive).

 Exercise 8   Write a method `Sum` that computes a similar result as in Exercise 6.

3.5. Types and Pattern Matching

Although Dafny is based on Hoare logic (as we will later see), it also includes some properties of type theory,[2] such as defining new data types.

---

[2] We will talk more about type theory in Section 4.2.

 Definition 3   A **binary tree** is a way to represent data hierarchically.

It is defined by the two constructors:

- Leaf, which has no values

- Node, which holds a value and points to two other trees (which can be either Nodes or Leafs)

The data structure expressed in BNF (Backus-Naur form)[3] is

```
1  tree ::= leaf | node nat tree tree
```

Trees are a very powerful structure in general – they can be used to represent mathematical proofs and even computation.

For example, the expression node 2 node(1 leaf leaf) node(3 leaf leaf)) represents the tree:

```
1    2
2   / \
3  1   3
```

As another example, here's a proof tree that describes the proof that given *A* and *B*, we can conclude *A* ∧ *B*:

```
1    A&B
2   /  \ (and)
3  A    B
```

---

[3] Backus-Naur is a notation for specifying syntaxes. It allows specifying syntax with sums (|) and products (). For example, foo ::= 1 | 2 specifies that foo can be either 1 or 2, and baz = <foo>2 specifies that baz can be either 12 or 22.

Here's another tree that represents the computation 1 + 2:

```
1    +
2   / \
3  1   2
```

To define such types in Dafny, we use the keyword datatype as follows:

```
1 datatype Tree<T> = Leaf | Node(T, Tree, Tree)
```

This code creates a new type constructor Tree T (it can be Tree int, Tree nat, etc.) with the value constructors Leaf and Node. Leaf is a constructor (function) that takes no arguments, and Node is a constructor that takes three arguments: the value of T (int, nat, etc.), a Tree (left), and another Tree (right). This corresponds to Definition 3.

Optionally, arguments within the value constructors can also be named; doing so will allow for easy destructing (retrieval) of the same.

```
1 datatype Tree<T> = Leaf | Node(value : T, left : Tree,
  right : Tree)
```

A much simpler (though limiting) definition would be to define a Tree just for natural numbers:

```
1 datatype TreeNat = Leaf | Node(nat, TreeNat, TreeNat)
```

Pattern matching is another crucial concept, especially in doing some computation by traversing (walking through) recursive data types such as Tree.

```
1 match(t)
2 {
3   case Leaf => ...
4   case Node(x, left, right) => ...
5   ...
6 }
```

This is just if-then-else in disguise, where a specific expression is matched (compared) to some values. When a value is matched, the corresponding case is returned.

For example, we can construct the following function that checks if a given element is contained in a Tree:

```
1   datatype Tree<T> = Leaf | Node(T, Tree, Tree)
2
3   function Contains<T>(t : Tree, v : T) : bool
4     decreases t
5   {
6     match t {
7       case Leaf => false
8       case Node(x, left, right) =>
9         if x == v then true else
10            if Contains(left, v) then true else
11              if Contains(right, v) then true else false
12    }
13  }
```

This function will recursively "walk" through a given Tree, and we say that the element v will be contained in this tree only if x == v for any x in that Tree.

For instance, for the value Node(1, Node(2, Leaf, Leaf), Node(3, Leaf, Leaf)), it will evaluate the following:

```
1  Contains(Node(1, Node(2, Leaf, Leaf), Node(3, Leaf,
       Leaf)), 3) ->
2  if 1 == 3 then true else
3  if Contains(Node(2, Leaf, Leaf), 3) then true else
4  if Contains(Node(3, Leaf, Leaf), 3) then true else false
```

where

```
 1  // This evaluates to false
 2  Contains(Node(2, Leaf, Leaf), 3) ->
 3  if 2 == 3 then true else
 4  if Contains(Leaf, 3) then true else
 5  if Contains(Leaf, 3) then true else false
 6
 7  // This evaluates to true
 8  Contains(Node(3, Leaf, Leaf), 3) ->
 9  if 3 == 3 then true else // specifically, this
10  if Contains(Leaf, 3) then true else
11  if Contains(Leaf, 3) then true else false
```

Thus, the final result will be true because of the expression
Contains(Node(3, Leaf, Leaf), 3).

For another simpler example, here is one way to represent natural
numbers:

```
1  datatype Nat = Z | S(Nat)
```

This defines two value constructors: Z (which does not accept any
arguments) and S (successor, which accepts a Nat). The number 0
corresponds to Z, the number 1 corresponds to S(Z), the number 2 to
S(S(Z)), etc.

Besides defining our own types, as we've seen, Dafny has a couple
of built-in data types: nat (for natural numbers), int (for integers), bool
(booleans), string (list of characters), etc.

We conclude this section by observing how we can represent powerful
computation by combining recursion, data types, and pattern matching.

Exercise 9   Implement a function NatTonat that takes a

Nat and returns a nat.

Hint: There are two cases to consider: Z, which corresponds to 0, and S(n), which corresponds to 1 + NatTonat(n).

 Exercise 10   Implement a function natToNat that takes a

nat and returns a Nat.

Hint: There are two cases to consider: 0, which corresponds to Z, and n, which corresponds to S(natToNat(n-1)).

 Exercise 11   Confirm that your functions work as they

should by adding the following method and making sure that Dafny compiles without errors:

```
1  method ExampleProof()
2    ensures natToNat(4) == S(S(S(S(Z))))
3    ensures NatTonat(S(S(S(S(Z))))) == 4
4  {}
```

CHAPTER 4

Mathematical Foundations

In this chapter, we will briefly cover two of the most important mathematical theories: set theory and type theory.

4.1. Set Theory

Set theory is often taken as the foundation of mathematics, depending on the nature of the problem being solved.

 Definition 1 Set theory is a formal system based on **sets**, which are actually a collection of objects.

As in programming, building abstractions in mathematics is of equal importance. The best way to understand something is to understand the atoms that make it up, individually. We will explain the theory from the lowest level to the highest – from the most basic object (the unordered collection) up to the definition of functions.

A set is an **unordered** collection of objects (elements). These objects can represent anything. A set can be either finite or infinite.

© Boro Sitnikovski 2022
B. Sitnikovski, *Introducing Software Verification with Dafny Language*,
https://doi.org/10.1007/978-1-4842-7978-6_4

Finite sets can be denoted by *roster notation*; we write out a list of objects contained in the set, separated by commas, and enclose them using curly braces. For example, one set of fruits is {apple, banana}. Since it is an unordered collection, we have that {apple, banana} = {banana, apple}.

Dafny has a built-in data type set. We construct sets as follows:

```
1  method Example()
2  {
3    var s1 : set<nat> := {}; // the empty set
4    var s2 : set<string> := {"apple", "banana"};
5  }
```

ⓘ   Definition 2   Membership of a set represents when a given object belongs to a set. It is denoted using the symbol $\in$.

For example, apple $\in$ {apple, banana} indicates that apple belongs to that set. In Dafny:

```
1  method Example()
2  {
3    var s1 : set<string> := {"apple", "banana"};
4    assert "apple" in s1; // Membership
5    assert |s1| == 2; // Length
6  }
```

ⓘ   Definition 3   An n-tuple is an **ordered collection** of n objects. As with sets, the objects can be anything. Tuples are usually denoted by a comma separating the list of objects and enclosing them using parentheses.

For example, $(a_1, a_2, ..., a_n)$ is one ordered collection, and we can use the set $\{\{1, \{a_1\}\}, \{2, \{a_2\}\}, ... , \{n, \{a_n\}\}\}$ to represent it.

This will allow us to extract the k-th element of the tuple, by picking x such that $\{k, \{x\}\} \in A$. Having done that, we now have that $(a, b) = (c, d) \equiv a = c \wedge b = d$, that is, two tuples are equal iff their first and second elements, respectively, are equal, and this is what makes them ordered.

An example of a tuple is (1 pm, 2 pm, 3 pm), which represents 3 hours in a given day, sequentially.

In Dafny, these ordered collections are represented with the seq type.

```
1  method Example()
2  {
3    var s1 : seq<string> := ["apple", "banana"];
4    assert "apple" in s1; // Membership
5    assert s1 == ["apple"] + ["banana"]; // Order
6    assert s1[0] == "apple"; // Access element
7    assert s1[0..1] == ["apple"]; // Subsequence
8    assert |s1| == 2; // Length
9  }
```

Roster notation is inconvenient for large sets, and it is impossible to use it for infinite sets. Another way to construct sets is by using the so-called *set-builder notation*. This notation specifies a set by assigning a predicate that satisfies all elements. It is typically of the form $\{x \mid P(x)\}$ where P is a predicate. If a is a specific object, then $a \in \{x \mid P(x)\}$ is true when $P(a)$ is true.

The syntax is similar in Dafny:

```
1  method Example()
2  {
3    assert (set x | x in {1, 2, 3} && x < 3) == {1, 2};
4  }
```

Definition 4   Cartesian product is defined as the set $\{(a, b)$
$\mid a \in A \land b \in B\}$. It is denoted $A \times B$.

For example, if $A = \{a, b\}$ and $B = \{1, 2, 3\}$, then the Cartesian product
represents the following set: $A \times B = \{(a, 1), (a, 2), (a, 3), (b, 1), (b, 2), (b, 3)\}$.

 Definition 5 A is a **subset** of B if all elements of A are in B
(but not necessarily vice versa). It is denoted as $A \subseteq B$, where
$A \subseteq B \leftrightarrow x \in A \rightarrow x \in B$.

For example, the expressions $\{1, 2\} \subseteq \{1, 2, 3\}$ and $\{1, 2, 3\} \subseteq \{1, 2, 3\}$ are
true. But this expression is not true: $\{1, 2, 3\} \subseteq \{1, 2\}$.

```
1  method Example()
2  {
3    assert {1, 2, 3} <= {1, 2, 3};
4    assert !({1, 2, 3} <= {1, 2});
5  }
```

Several other set operations can be defined using logical operations:

1. Union: $A \cup B = \{x \mid x \in A \lor x \in B\}$

2. Intersection: $A \cap B = \{x \mid x \in A \land x \in B\}$

3. Difference: $A \setminus B = \{x \mid x \in A \land x \notin B\}$

In Dafny, we can represent these as follows:

```
1  predicate Union<T>(a : set<T>, b : set<T>, el : T)
2  {
3    el in a || el in b <==> el in a + b
4  }
```

```
 5
 6  predicate Intersection<T>(a : set<T>, b : set<T>, el : T)
 7  {
 8     el in a && el in b <==> el in a * b
 9  }
10
11  predicate Difference<T>(a : set<T>, b : set<T>, el : T)
12  {
13     el in a && !(el in b) <==> el in a - b
14  }
```

with the following examples:

1. $\{1, 2, 3\} \cup \{1, 2\} = \{1, 2, 3\}$

2. $\{1, 2, 3\} \cap \{1, 2\} = \{1, 2\}$

3. $\{1, 2, 3\} \setminus \{1, 2\} = \{3\}$

```
1  method Example()
2  {
3     assert {1, 2, 3} + {1, 2} == {1, 2, 3};
4     assert {1, 2, 3} * {1, 2} == {1, 2};
5     assert {1, 2, 3} - {1, 2} == {3};
6  }
```

ⓘ **Definition 6** **Relation** R is defined as a subset of the Cartesian product of two sets, that is, $R \subseteq A \times B$.

For example, the relation "greater than" is a relation for the following set: {(cat, mouse), (mouse, cheese), (cat, cheese)}. To denote that $(a, b) \in R$, we write aRb, that is, $aRb \leftrightarrow (a, b) \in R$. Thus, we have that cat R mouse, since a cat is greater than a mouse.

Definition 7   A **function** f is defined as a relation between A and B if exactly one element of the second set is assigned to each element of the first set. For this mapping, it is valid that $f \subseteq A \times B$ and $f : A \rightarrow B$.

In other words, a function is a subset of all combinations of ordered pairs whose first element is A and whose second element is B.[1] The relation R defined earlier is not a function, since "cat" maps to two different values.

For example, $f(x) = x + 1$ is a function that for a given number returns the same number increased by one. It holds that $f(1) = 2$, $f(2) = 3$, etc. Another way to represent this function is to use sets: $f = \{(1, 2), (2, 3), (3, 4), ...\}$. A third way to represent functions is in the form of a table. The function $f(x)$ that receives an argument x is represented in a two-column table, where the first column is the input and the second column is the output. The function $f(x, y)$ that accepts two arguments, x and y, is represented by a table with three columns, where the first and second columns represent the input and the third column the output, and so on. Thus, the function $f(x) = x+1$ represented in tabular form would look like Table 4-1.

Table 4-1. *Example of a function*

x	f(x)
1	2
2	3
...	...

---

[1] In set theory, the predicate P is a function (relational subset), $P \subseteq A \times \{\top, \bot\}$, where A is a set of inputs, and the output is either true or false. This may not be the case with other systems, such as first-order logic, in which $P(A)$, $P(B)$, etc., are atomic expressions instead of mathematical functions. This is what makes first-order logic independent of set theory.

4.2. Type Theory

As a motivation for the need for type theory, we will present **Russell's paradox**, according to the mathematician Bertrand Russell:

> In a village in which there is only one barber, there is a rule according to which the barber shaves everyone who doesn't shave themselves, and no one else. Now, who shaves the barber?

- Suppose the barber shaves himself. Then, he's one of those who shave themselves, but the barber shaves only those who don't shave themselves, which is a contradiction.

- Alternatively, if we assume that the barber doesn't shave himself, then he is in the group of people whom the barber shaves, which again is a contradiction.

- Thus, the barber doesn't shave himself, but he also doesn't *not* shave himself – a paradox.

Some set theories are affected by Russell's paradox. As a response to this, between 1902 and 1908, Bertrand Russell himself proposed different type theories as an attempt to resolve the issue. By joining types to values, we avoid the paradox because in this theory every set is defined as having elements from a distinct type, for example, Type 1. Elements from Type 1 can be included in a different set, say, elements of Type 2, and so forth. Thus, the paradox is no longer an issue since the set of elements of Type 1 cannot be contained in their own set, since the types do not match. In a way, we're adding hierarchy to sets in order to resolve the issue of "self-referential" sets.

> **ℹ Definition 1**   Type theory is defined as a class of formal systems. In these theories, every object is joined with a type, and operations upon these objects are constrained by the joined types. In order to say that x is of type X, we denote x : X. Very often, functions are a primitive concept in type theory, unlike set theory, where they are defined in terms of relations.

For example, with 1 : nat, 2 : nat, we say that 1 and 2 are of type nat, that is, natural numbers. A function + : nat $\rightarrow$ nat $\rightarrow$ nat takes two objects of type nat and returns an object of type nat.

As we've seen in Section 3.5, we can define these in Dafny as follows:

```
1  method Main()
2  {
3    var one : nat := 1;
4  }
5
6  function Plus(a : nat, b : nat) : nat
7  {
8    // ...
9  }
```

> **ℹ Definition 2**   In type theory, a **type constructor** is a function that constructs new types from existing ones; that is, it accepts types as input and returns types as output. A **value constructor** is a function that constructs values for given types.

Recall the definition of Tree in 3.5. As we discussed, Leaf and Node are value constructors, and Tree is a type constructor.

```
1  datatype Tree<T> = Leaf | Node(T, Tree, Tree)
```

Algebraic data types are complex types, that is, types constructed by combining other types. Two classes of algebraic types are **sum** and **product**.

 Definition 3   Algebraic data types are types where we can

additionally specify the form for each of the elements. They are called "algebraic" in the sense that the types are constructed using algebraic operations. The algebra here is sum and product:

- Sum (union) is an alternation. It is denoted as A | B, and it means that a constructed value is either of type A or B.

- Product is a combination. It is denoted as A B, and it means that a constructed value is a pair where the first element is of type A and the second element is of type B.

To understand the algebra they capture, we denote with $|A|$ the number of possible values of type A. When we create an algebraic sum, we have $|A \mid B| = |A| + |B|$. Similarly, for an algebraic product, we have $|A\,B| = |A| \cdot |B|$.

As an example, assume that we have two types: nat for natural numbers and real for real numbers.

- Using sum (union), we can construct a new type nat | real. Valid values of this type are 1 : nat | real, 3.14 : nat | real, etc.

- Using product, we can construct a new type nat real. Valid values of this type are 1 1.5 : nat real, 2 3.14 : nat real, etc.

For another example, consider the type bool that has two possible values: *true* and *false*. Thus, |bool| = 2. The type Unit has one possible value: *Unit*.

```
1  datatype Unit = Unit
```

We can now form a sum type bool | Unit that has length 3 with values *true*, *false*, *Unit*.

```
1  datatype MyTypeSum = MyTypen(bool) | MyTyper(Unit)
2
3  method Main()
4  {
5    var first : MyTypeSum := MyTypen(true);
6    var second : MyTypeSum := MyTypen(false);
7    var third : MyTypeSum := MyTyper(Unit);
8  }
```

Additionally, the product type bool Unit is of length 2 with the values *true Unit*, *false Unit*.

```
1  datatype MyTypeProduct = MyTypeProduct(bool, Unit)
2
3  method Main()
4  {
5    var first : MyTypeProduct := MyTypeProduct(true, Unit);
6    var second : MyTypeProduct := MyTypeProduct(false, Unit);
7  }
```

As we showed, sums and products can be combined to form more complex data structures.

CHAPTER 5

Proofs

In this chapter, we'll dive deeper into mathematical proofs to get us prepared for applying them to prove software correctness within Dafny.

We will start with the most basic concept: **substitution**. It lies at the core of mathematics and, as such, plays an important role in mathematical proofs. Substitution consists of a systematic replacement of the appearances of a symbol with a certain value, and it can be applied in a variety of contexts involving formal systems.

ℹ Definition 1 In an expression P, the variable x is called **free** if it does not appear anywhere in P. Otherwise, if it does appear, then it is called **bound**.

For example, $x > 2$ is a subformula of the expression $\forall x, x > 2$. The variable x is bound to $x > 2$ (from the $\forall$). However, in the expression $f(x) = x + y$, x is again bound by $f(x)$, but y is a free variable because it does not appear in $f(x)$.

ℹ Definition 2 **Substitution** is denoted by $P[E/x]$ and is defined such that in the expression P, every free occurrence of x is replaced by E.

For example, if the following is given:

1. Inference rule: If $a = b$ and $b = c$, then $a = c$

2. Two axioms: $1 = 2$ and $2 = 3$

then the following can be "proved":

1. $1 = 2$ (axiom)

2. $2 = 3$ (axiom)

3. $1 = 2$ and $2 = 3$ (from 1 and 2 combined)

4. $1 = 3$ (from 3 and the inference rule)

It is known that $1 = 3$ does not make sense, but in the context of the aforementioned, this proof is valid.

Essentially, we applied substitution given some inference rule, concretizing the values within the rule. More specifically, we substituted a for 1, b for 2, and c for 3 within the expression "If $a = b$ and $b = c$, then $a = c$".

> **ℹ** **Definition 3   A mathematical argument** consists of a set of statements. Mathematical arguments are used to prove that a given statement is true or false.

> **ℹ** **Definition 4   Proof** is an inferential argument for a set of given mathematical propositions. To prove a mathematical fact, it must be shown that the conclusion (the goal being proved) logically follows from the hypothesis (the set of given propositions).

For example, to prove that G follows from a set of statements (mathematical argument) $\{g_1, g_2, \ldots, g_n\}$, it must be shown that $(g_1 \wedge g_2 \wedge \ldots \wedge g_n) \to G$[1].

A direct consequence of Definition 4 is the following definition.

 Definition 5   A mathematical argument is **valid** if and only if in the case where all of the propositions are true, the conclusion is also true.

At the lowest level (formal system), a proof is just a transformation (substitution) from one expression to another. At higher levels, however, how proofs are done depends on the symbols and the operations on them. For example, since there is $\wedge$ in logic, certain rules can be used to introduce/eliminate it.

5.1. Proofs by Truth Tables

We consider the following statement as an example: from $A \wedge B$, we can conclude that B is true, for **any values** of A and B. To prove this, one proof technique that can be used is constructing a **truth table**. Truth tables are represented by breaking down a given statement into subformulas until it can no longer be separated (atoms), and each subformula is included in a column.

---

[1] Note that implication was used in the context of mathematical proof. There is another symbol similar to the implication, the symbol $\vdash$ that has a similar meaning, but this symbol is at the meta-level instead of the object level as the implication, and we will cover it in Section 5.4.

Table 5-1. *An example proof using truth tables*

A	B	$A \land B$
T	T	T
T	⊥	⊥
⊥	T	⊥
⊥	⊥	⊥

Note that wherever $A \land B$ is true (the set of given propositions, or premises, or hypothesis), then so is B (the conclusion), which means that this is a valid logical argument according to Definition 5.

In Dafny, we can represent the same proof using the following code:

```
1  predicate Statement1(a : bool, b : bool)
2  {
3    a && b ==> b
4  }
5
6  method Example1()
7    ensures forall a, b :: Statement(a, b)
8  {}
```

 Exercise 1   Construct a truth table for the statement "from A we can conclude $A \lor B$". Is the proof valid?

 Exercise 2   Construct a truth table for the statement "from A we can conclude B". Is the proof valid?

Exercise 3   Construct a truth table for the statement "from *A* and *B* we can conclude *B*". Is the proof valid?

 Exercise 4   Write out the code in Dafny for the previous exercises.

5.2. Three-Column Proofs

There are several ways to do mathematical proofs. Another one of them is by using the so-called three-column proofs. For this technique, we construct a table with three columns: the number of the current step, step (or expression derived), and reasoning (explanation of how we got to the particular step).

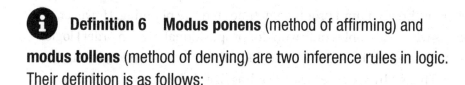 **Definition 6   Modus ponens** (method of affirming) and **modus tollens** (method of denying) are two inference rules in logic. Their definition is as follows:

- Modus ponens states: If we are given $p \rightarrow q$ and p, then we can conclude q.

- Modus tollens states: If we are given $p \rightarrow q$ and $\neg q$, then we can conclude $\neg p$.

For example, given $A \vee B$, $B \rightarrow C$, $\neg C$, prove A. We do the proof as follows.

Table 5-2. *An example proof using three-column proofs*

No.	Step	Reasoning
1	$A \lor B$	Given
2	$B \to C$	Given
3	$\neg C$	Given
4	$(B \to C) \land \neg C$	2 and 3
5	$\neg B$	Modus tollens rule on 4, that is, $(p \to q \land \neg q) \to \neg p$
6	$(A \lor B) \land \neg B$	1 and 5
7	$(A \land \neg B) \lor (B \land \neg B)$	6 and distributive law
8	$A \land \neg B$	7, where $p \land \neg p$ is a contradiction
9	A	8

Proofs with truth tables look much simpler than three-column proofs. Truth tables simply substitute variables with a value ($\top$ or $\bot$) and simplify, whereas three-column proofs sometimes require planning. However, proofs with truth tables only work for propositional (zeroth order) logic – the table method is essentially the decidability algorithm for zeroth-order logic. That's why they are easy (if verbose) and always work and why column proofs become necessary once we start using quantifiers.

Here's the same proof in Dafny – it automatically takes care of all the reasoning for us.

```
1  predicate Statement2(a : bool, b : bool, c : bool)
2  {
3      (a || b) && (b ==> c) && (! c) ==> a
4  }
5
```

```
6  method Example2()
7    ensures forall a, b, c :: Statement2(a, b, c)
8  {}
```

Exercise 5   Prove, by means of three-column proof, the statement "from $A \to B$ and $A \land C$, we can conclude B".

Exercise 6   Prove, by means of three-column proof, the statement "from $A \to B$ and $\neg B \land \neg C$, we can conclude $\neg A$".

5.3. Formal Proofs

We've seen how we can construct proofs with truth tables. However, if our statements involve the use of quantifiers, then doing proofs with truth tables is impossible. Three-column proofs, in contrast, contain many details. Ideally, the proof should be short, clear, and concise about what we want to prove. Therefore, we will try to prove a statement using formal proof.

To prove $A \land B \to B$, we start by assuming that $A \land B$ is true since otherwise, the statement is vacuously true (true by default) by definition of implication (check the truth table for implication in Chapter 2). If $A \land B$ is true, then both A and B are true by definition of $\land$, that is, we can conclude B.

Do not worry if the previous paragraph sounded too magical, there is not much magic involved. Usually, it comes down to using a few rules for how we can use given information and achieve our goal. We summarize these rules next.

Table 5-3. *Proving goals of form*

Goal form	Technique
$P \to Q$	Assume that P is true and prove Q
$\neg P$	Assume that P is true and arrive at a contradiction
$P_1 \wedge P_2 \wedge \ldots \wedge P_n$	Prove each one of $P_1, P_2, \ldots, P_n$ separately
$P_1 \vee P_2 \vee \ldots \vee P_n$	Prove that at least one of $P_1, P_2, \ldots, P_n$
$P \leftrightarrow Q$	Prove both $P \to Q$ and $Q \to P$
$\forall x, P(x)$	Assume that x is an arbitrary object and prove that $P(x)$
$\exists x, P(x)$	Find an x such that $P(x)$ is true
$\exists! x, P(x)^2$	Prove $\exists x, P(x)$ (existence) and $\forall x \forall y, (P(x) \wedge P(y) \to x = y)$ (uniqueness) separately

Table 5-4. *Using givens of form*

Given form	Technique
$P \to Q$	If P is also given, then conclude that Q (by modus ponens)
$\neg P$	If P can be proven true, then conclude a contradiction
$P_1 \wedge P_2 \wedge \ldots \wedge P_n$	Treat each one of $P_1, P_2, \ldots, P_n$ as a given
$P_1 \vee P_2 \vee \ldots \vee P_n$	Use proof by cases, where in each case you assume one of $P_1, P_2, \ldots, P_n$
$P \leftrightarrow Q$	Conclude both $P \to Q$ and $Q \to P$
$\forall x, P(x)$	For any x, conclude that $P(x)$
$\exists x, P(x)$	Introduce a new variable, say, x_0, so that $P(x_0)$ is true
$\exists! x, P(x)$	Introduce a new variable, say, x_1, so that $P(x_1)$ is true. Can also use that $\forall x \forall y, (P(x) \wedge P(y) \to x = y)$

---

[2] The notation $\exists!$ represents that **exactly one** object satisfies the predicate.

For example, we can use these techniques to do the following proofs:

1. $A \wedge B \rightarrow A \vee B$: To prove this goal, we will assume $A \wedge B$ and use proof by cases:

    1. Proof for A: Since we're given $A \wedge B$, we are also given A. Thus, A.

    2. Proof for B: Since we're given $A \wedge B$, we are also given B. Thus, B.

    3. Thus, $A \vee B$.

2. $A \wedge B \leftrightarrow B \wedge A$: To prove this goal, we will prove both sides for the implications:

    1. Proof for $A \wedge B \rightarrow B \wedge A$: We can assume that $A \wedge B$; thus, we have both A and B. To prove the goal of $B \wedge A$, we need to prove B and A separately, which we already have as given.

    2. Proof for $B \wedge A \rightarrow A \wedge B$: We can assume that $B \wedge A$; thus, we have both B and A. To prove the goal of $A \wedge B$, we need to prove A and B separately, which we already have as given.

    3. Thus, $A \wedge B \leftrightarrow B \wedge A$.

3. $\forall x, x = x$: We know that for any number x, that number is equal to itself. Thus, $\forall x, x = x$.

4. $\exists x, x > 0$: To prove this, we only need to find an x such that it is greater than 0. One valid example is 1. Thus, $\exists x, x > 0$.

Exercise 7   Prove the proofs from the previous exercises by means of a formal proof (similarly to the proofs given in this section).

5.4. Sequent Calculus Notation

Sequent calculus is a notation for mathematical logic, especially used in some theories, such as Hoare's logic (which we will talk about later). Each expression is derived (via inference rules) from a previous expression.

In the following expression, the hypothesis is A, and the conclusion is B. The fraction represents an implication that from A, it follows B, at the meta-level.

$$\frac{A}{B}$$

In the next expression, the hypothesis is A and B, and the conclusion is C. That is, from A and B, it follows C. Presented in the previous notation discussed, this can be seen as $A \wedge B \rightarrow C$ (object level), whereas the sequent notation represents it at the meta-level.

$$\frac{A \quad B}{C}$$

An environment Γ is defined as a list of statements. The following expression states that the statement $x = 3$ belongs in some environment Γ:

$$x = 3 \in \Gamma$$

The next expression indicates that a given environment Γ proves that $x = 3$:

$$\Gamma \vdash x = 3$$

The next expression indicates that when $x = 3$ is in some environment Γ, then Γ proves that $x = 3$.

$$\frac{x = 3 \in \Gamma}{\Gamma \vdash x = 3}$$

For example, here are the logical rules for disjunction expressed with this notation:

$$\frac{A}{A \vee B}(1) \quad \frac{A \rightarrow B \quad C \rightarrow B \quad A \vee C}{B}(2)$$

And the logical rules for implication (modus ponens in disguise):

$$\frac{A \quad A \rightarrow B}{B}$$

And finally, here's how we can represent the logical rules of conjunction: left elimination, right elimination, and introduction, respectively:

$$\frac{A \wedge B}{A}(1) \quad \frac{A \wedge B}{B}(2) \quad \frac{A \quad B}{A \wedge B}(3)$$

Together with an example proof that from $A \wedge B$, we can conclude $B \wedge A$:

$$\frac{\dfrac{A \wedge B(given)}{B}(2) \quad \dfrac{A \wedge B(given)}{A}(1)}{B \wedge A}$$

Note that this is a proof tree that corresponds to the Tree definition in Section 3.5.

 Exercise 8   Prove the proofs from the previous exercises using sequent calculus notation.

5.5. Example: Proving a Mathematical Property

In the following example, we will prove the mathematical property:

$$\min(a - c, b - c) = \min(a, b) - c$$

The function min is defined as follows:

$$\min(a,b) = \begin{cases} a & \text{if } a<b, \\ b & \text{otherwise} \end{cases}$$

In Dafny, it can be defined as

```
1  function Min(a : int, b : int) : int
2  {
3    if a < b then a else b
4  }
```

After defining the function, the proof follows. It is simply

```
1  method Example()
2  {
3    assert forall a, b, c :: Min(a - c, b - c) ==
       Min(a, b) - c;
4  }
```

The following message is returned from Dafny:

```
1  Dafny program verifier finished with 3 verified, 0 errors
2  Program compiled successfully
```

With that, the proof is complete. To prove this mathematically, we use proof by cases:

1. Case $a - c > b - c$: It's true that $\min(a - c, b - c) = b - c$, and from $a - c > b - c$, it follows that $a > b$, that is, $\min(a, b) = b$. Thus, $b - c = b - c$.

2. Case $a - c \leq b - c$: It's true that $\min(a - c, b - c) = a - c$, and from $a - c < b - c$, it follows that $a < b$, that is, $\min(a, b) = a$. Thus, $a - c = a - c$.

With these two cases, it can be concluded that $\min(a-c, b- c) = \min(a, b) - c$.

CHAPTER 6

Specifications

Specifications, as a special form of computation, allow us to be precise by verifying that some existing computation performs the desired result. In this chapter, we will cover the details behind specifications.

6.1. Hoare Logic

ⓘ **Definition 1** **Hoare logic** is a formal system that allows to reason about the correctness of computer programs. The key feature of Hoare logic is the **Hoare triple** {P}C{Q} where

- C is a command in a programming language

- P is a precondition (predicate that is true before C is executed)

- Q is a postcondition (predicate that is true after C was executed)

© Boro Sitnikovski 2022
B. Sitnikovski, *Introducing Software Verification with Dafny Language*,
https://doi.org/10.1007/978-1-4842-7978-6_6

Here are a few examples of such triples:

- $\{x + 1 = 43\}y := x + 1\{y = 43\}$, that is, if $x + 1 = 43$ is true before $y := x + 1$ is executed, then after the execution of this command, $y = 43$ will be true.

- $\{x + 1 \leq N\}x := x + 1\{x \leq N\}$, that is, if $x + 1 \leq N$ is true before x is increased by 1, then $x \leq N$ will be true after the increase.

We show the inference rules of this system, before giving a few examples.

Table 6-1. *Inference rules of Hoare logic*

Rule	Formula
Empty	$\{P\}\,\mathbf{skip}\,\{P\}$
Assignment	$\{P[E\,/\,x]\}\,x := E\,\{P\}$
Composition	$\dfrac{\{P\}S\{Q\}\ \{Q\}T\{R\}}{\{P\}S;T\{R\}}$
Conditional	$\dfrac{\{B \wedge P\}S\{Q\}\,\{\neg B \wedge P\}T\{Q\}}{\{P\}\,\mathbf{if}\ B\ \mathbf{then}\ S\ \mathbf{else}\ T\ \mathbf{endif}\,\{Q\}}$
Consequence	$\dfrac{P_1 \rightarrow P_2\ \{P_2\}S\{Q_2\}\ Q_2 \rightarrow Q_1}{\{P_1\}S\{Q_1\}}$
"While"[1]	$\dfrac{\{P \wedge B\}S\{P\}}{\{P\}\,\mathbf{while}\ B\ \mathbf{do}\ S\ \mathbf{done}\,\{\neg B \wedge P\}}$

For example, if we are given the following (from the rule of assignment):

---

[1] This rule represents an invariant.

$$\{x + 1 = 43\}y := x + 1\{y = 43\}$$

$$\{y = 43\}z := y\{z = 43\}$$

then, according to the rule of composition, we can conclude

$$\{x + 1 = 43\}y := x + 1; z := y\{z = 43\}$$

For another example, to prove

$$\{x \leq 10\}\textbf{while } x < 10 \textbf{ do } x := x + 1 \textbf{ done}\{\neg(x < 10) \wedge x \leq 10\}$$

we can use the "While" rule, first proving the hypothesis part:

$$\{x < 10\}x := x + 1\{x \leq 10\}$$

which follows from the assignment rule. Finally, the postcondition $\{\neg(x < 10) \wedge x \leq 10\}$ can be simplified to $\{x = 10\}$.

For a more detailed example, consider the statements $c := a$; $a := b$; $b := c$.

We can invoke the assignment rule in all three cases:

1.   Substitute x with c, E with a, and P with $c = d \wedge b = e$ to get to $\{a = d \wedge b = e\}c := a; \{a = d \wedge b = e\}$.

2.   Substitute x with a, E with b, and P with $c = d \wedge a = e$ to get to $\{c = d \wedge b = e\}a := b; \{c = d \wedge a = e\}$.

3.   Substitute x with b, E with c, and P with $b = d \wedge a = e$ to get to $\{c = d \wedge a = e\}b := c; \{b = d \wedge a = e\}$.

4.   Finally, use the rule of composition to get to $\{a = d \wedge b = e\}c := a; a := b; b := c; \{b = d \wedge a = e\}$.

Now, if we ignore the "program" part of that last Hoare triple and focus solely on the specifications part, we get that $a = d \wedge b = e \rightarrow b = d \wedge a = e$. That is, the command swaps the values of a and b.

In a nutshell, Hoare logic allows us to "translate" a piece of code into the language of mathematical logic; that is, Hoare logic maps a sequence of program statements into an expression of first-order logic. As we've seen, this enables us to ignore the *program* part in and only focus on the *specifications* since in most cases, it will be immediately obvious what the program is calculating just by looking at its specifications. This is very similar to the explicitness of the PowerMethod method vs. the Power function that we discussed in Chapter 3.

A good learning exercise is to implement Hoare logic yourself or any other formal system for that matter.[2] One such tutorial can be found in [7] where Hoare logic is implemented using the Haskell programming language.

 Exercise 1 On paper, using Hoare logic, prove that the empty statement does not alter the value of a, that is, $a = d$ before and after the execution of the command.

 Exercise 2 On paper, using Hoare logic, prove that the statement $x := 0$ produces a postcondition that x is between 0 and 15, that is, $0 \leq x \leq 15$.

Hint: Set P to $0 \leq x \leq 15$ and ensure that the precondition is true.

---

[2] We will show an example implementation of a toy formal system in Chapter 9.

6.2. Z3 and Dafny

Knowing how these proofs work, in theory, provides a good understanding of what Dafny does behind the curtains to prove stuff. But imagine if we had to do all proofs manually, just like we did in the previous section – it will take us a very long time to prove even the most basic properties of computer programs.

For this, computers are here to help us, more specifically Z3 – an automated theorem prover that uses some smart techniques to prove formulas automatically.

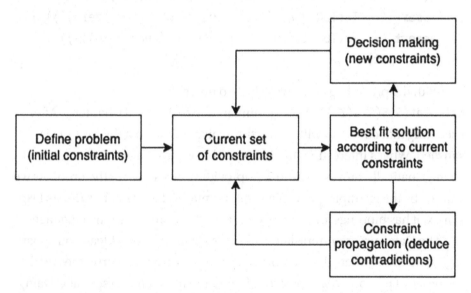

Figure 6-1. *Constraint programming*

Z3 uses concepts from a programming paradigm called **constraint programming**,[3] and the general, high-level algorithm is briefly described in Figure 6-1. It is developed by Microsoft, and the first release was made in 2012. It is still in active development and is heavily used in the industry.

```
1  (declare-datatypes () ((Nat
2    zero (succ (pred Nat)))))
3  (define-fun-rec IntToNat ((n Int)) Nat
4    (ite (= n 0) zero (succ (IntToNat (- n 1)))))
5  (define-fun-rec NatToInt ((n Nat)) Int
6    (ite (= n zero) 0 (+ 1 (NatToInt (pred n)))))
7  (assert (= (IntToNat 4) (succ (succ (succ (succ zero))))))
8  (assert (= (NatToInt (succ (succ (succ (succ zero))))) 4))
9  (check-sat)
```

With the preceding code, we ask Z3 to prove that
NatToInt(S(S(S(S(Z))))) == 4, similar to Exercise 11 of Chapter 3. After executing that code,[4] Z3 will return sat, which means that the formula is satisfied. What's interesting in this case is that we just gave the formula, and Z3 automatically proves it without us providing any steps for the proof. As we can see by the example, Z3 uses a similar syntax to Lisp.[5] But besides its Lisp syntax, it has bindings for Python, C++, and other programming languages.

The Dafny programming language uses Z3 and borrows ideas from Hoare logic, and this is what allows automatic proving of program correctness with the usage of preconditions, postconditions, and invariants. Essentially, Dafny translates programs into Z3 equivalents and checks satisfiability.

---

[3] The key feature of this paradigm is using a backtracking algorithm, essentially recursing through a tree and filtering branches according to some condition. Think of searching in a maze, in an attempt to find the exit.

[4] Running Z3 programs within Dafny is not possible, though the interested reader can install Z3 and experiment with it.

[5] Lisp is a programming language with a fully parenthesized prefix notation in which lists are the main concept [13].

6.3. Preconditions and Postconditions

Preconditions are defined using the keyword `requires` between the declaration and the body. Considering `MultipleReturns` from Chapter 3:

```
1  method MultipleReturns(x : int, y : int) returns (more :
      int, less : int)
2    requires 0 < y
3  {
4    more := x + y;
5    less := x - y;
6  }
```

This method corresponds to the following Hoare triple:

$$\{0 < y\}more := x + y;\ less := x - \{\textbf{true}\}$$

As we've seen, postconditions are defined using the keyword ensures. Recalling the method Abs from Chapter 3, here's one valid postcondition:

```
1  method Abs(x : int) returns (y : int)
2    ensures 0 <= y
3  {
4    if x < 0
5    {
6      return -x;
7    }
8    else
9    {
10      return x;
11    }
12  }
```

This method corresponds to the Hoare triple:

$$\{0 \le 0\}x := Abs(x)\{0 \le x\}, \text{ or } \{\textbf{true}\}x := Abs(x)\{0 \le x\}$$

Preconditions and postconditions can be combined as follows:

```
1  method MultipleReturns(x : int, y : int) returns (more :
       int, less : int)
2    requires 0 < y
3    ensures less < x < more
4  {
5    more := x + y;
6    less := x - y;
7  }
```

This makes the Hoare triple:

$$\{0 < y\}more := x + y;\ less := x - y\{less < x < more\}$$

Dafny is automatically able to prove these triples, but if you want to prove them manually using pen and paper, you can use the rules of Hoare logic, as we did in Section 6.1.

6.4. Invariants

An **invariant** is a property that remains unchanged when applying some transformation rule within a formal system. It is especially useful for proving certain properties for loops.

If preconditions and postconditions show what the loop does before and after it's executed, then invariants show what the loop does **during** execution.

To give a small example, let's go back to the previous PowerMethod example and try to claim that the product x^n is a positive number at any point in computation (for x and n natural numbers). Consider the following code:

```
1  method PowerMethod(x : nat, n : nat) returns (p : nat)
2  {
3    p := 1;
4    var i := n;
5
6    while i != 0
7      invariant p >= 1
8    {
9      p := p * x;
10     i := i - 1;
11   }
12 }
```

We used the keyword `invariant` to state that `p >= 1` for every iteration of the loop. However, if we try to run this program, Dafny will complain that the loop does not maintain the invariant. While this is obvious at runtime, Dafny doesn't have enough information at compile time to deduce this fact. Adding the precondition that `x >= 1` fixes the issue.

For another example, we can prove that `PowerMethod` and `Power` are equivalent to each other by adding `invariant p == Power(x, n-i)` after line 6. This invariant states that for every iteration in the loop, it's true that `p == Power(x, n-i)`. That is, for `x = 2` and `n = 3`, it holds that

1. `1 == Power(2, 0)`

2. `2 == Power(2, 1)`

3. `4 == Power(2, 2)`

4. `8 == Power(2, 3)`

With this, the postcondition `ensures p == Power(x, n)` can be added to the verification part of `PowerMethod`. But note that if we try to add that code without the invariant being present, Dafny will not be able to automatically prove the claim.

Invariance in one way helps Dafny to prove a claim by "filling in" certain missing parts so that a specific proof can be completed. The trickiest bit is finding a loop invariant that's both maintained by the loop and also that lets us prove what we need after the loop is finished. Thinking in terms of Hoare logic may be helpful in this case.

For example, consider the PowerMethod from before, but instead of guessing the invariant, we will now try to guess the actual code, given the invariant. This gives the following Hoare triple:

$$\{p = Power(x, n - i)\}?; i := i - 1\{p = Power(x, n - (i - 1))\}$$

That is, $\{p = x^{n-i}\}?; i := i - 1\{p = x^{n-i+1}\}$; the precondition is before i was decreased, and the postcondition is after it was decreased. The only way a product can turn from x^{n-i} to $x^{(n-i)+1}$ is if we multiply it by another x. Thus, the statement is $p := p \cdot x$.

6.5. Arrays

Arrays are pretty similar to sequences (seq from Section 4.1), with the difference that they are mutable and the elements' values can change in an array.

```
1  method Example()
2  {
3    var a : array<string> := new string[] ["apple", "banana"];
4    assert a[0] == "apple"; // Access element
5    assert a[0..1] == ["apple"]; // Subsequence
6    assert a.Length == 2; // Length
7    a[0] := "orange"; // Assignment
8    assert a[0] == "orange";
9  }
```

For example, the following code expresses the idea that every element in a given array is a positive number:

```
1  forall k : int :: 0 <= k < a.Length ==> 0 < a[k]
```

Mathematically, it's the expression $\forall k \in a, 0 < k$.

For another example, we provide a method that calculates the sum of all elements in an array:

```
1   method SumArray(a : array<nat>) returns (sum : nat)
2      requires 0 < a.Length
3   {
4     var i := 0;
5     sum := 0;
6     while i < a.Length
7     {
8        sum := sum + a[i];
9        i := i + 1;
10    }
11  }
```

We have to use the precondition that 0 < a.Length, since otherwise we would get the error Error: index out of range we need to tell Dafny that we are surely working with non-empty lists.

We now test this method as follows:

```
1  method Main()
2  {
3    var example := new nat[] [1, 2];
4    var sum := SumArray(example);
5    print(sum);
6  }
```

Dafny will print 3, which is the sum of 1 and 2.

6.6. Termination

To talk about termination, as an example we consider the following code that represents a loop for i from 0 to n:

```
1  method Loop()
2  {
3    var i := 0;
4    var n := 20;
5    while i != n
6    {
7      i := i + 1;
8    }
9  }
```

In this case, Dafny will return the following error:

```
1  test.dfy(5,4): Error: cannot prove termination; try
       supplying a decreases clause for the loop
```

Loops in general pose a problem for Dafny. There is no way Dafny can automatically know whether a given loop will terminate. Using the keyword decreases will tell Dafny that a certain expression is converging to a base value. That is, if n - i decreases, then this loop will eventually stop; it will execute as long as i != n.

```
1  while i != n
2    invariant 0 <= i <= n
3    decreases n - i
4  {
5    i := i + 1;
6  }
```

We further had to state that i is limited between 0 and n; otherwise, Dafny would return the following error:

```
1  test.dfy(6,20): Error: decreases expression must be bounded
     below by 0 at end of loop iteration
```

For another example, consider the following function that gets the nearest previous even number:

```
1  function GetPreviousEven(n : nat) : nat
2    decreases n
3  {
4    if n == 0 then 1
5    else if (n - 1) % 2 == 0 then n - 1
6    else GetPreviousEven(n - 1)
7  }
```

That definition works fine. Now, let's try to do it the other way around – get the next even number instead of the previous:

```
1  function GetNextEven(n : nat) : nat
2    decreases n
3  {
4    if (n + 1) % 2 == 0 then n + 1
5    else GetNextEven(n + 1)
6  }
```

In this case, Dafny won't be able to prove the decreases clause because n isn't really decreasing. Instead, we need to rewrite our function as

```
1  function GetNextEven(n : nat, bound : nat) : nat
2    decreases bound - n
3  {
4    if n >= bound then 0
5    else if (n + 1) % 2 == 0 then n + 1
6    else GetNextEven(n + 1, bound)
7  }
```

We added an upper bound to the calculation process.

In general, recursive definitions have to be written in such a way that it's obvious to Dafny that they converge to the base case(s).

6.7. Example: Finding a Maximum Number in an Array

The following code defines a method that will find the maximum number in an array:

```
1  method FindMax(a : array<int>) returns (max : int)
2    requires 0 < a.Length
3  {
4    var i := 0;
5    max := a[0]; // Assume that the first element is
     the largest
6    while i < a.Length
7      decreases a.Length - i
8    {
9      if a[i] >= max
10     {
11         max := a[i];
12     }
13     i := i + 1;
14   }
15 }
```

Further, we will add some more specifications to demonstrate how quantifiers can be used. We claim that any array contains a largest element, that is:

$$\exists m \forall k \in a, k \leq m$$

The method's specifications are altered as follows:

```
1  method FindMax(a : array<int>) returns (max : int)
2    requires 0 < a.Length
3    ensures exists k :: (0 < k < a.Length ==> max == a[k])
4    ensures forall k :: (0 < k < a.Length ==> max >= a[k])
```

The two quantifiers are divided into two different expressions; the first expression indicates that there exists such maximum element, and the second expression indicates that all elements in the sequence are less than or equal to that maximum element. However, if the given code is executed, Dafny will return an error since the forall postcondition cannot be proven due to the lack of specifications in the while loop.

As before, if we help Dafny by entering the correct invariants into the loop, Dafny will be able to successfully prove the claim. Adding the following invariants completes the proof:

```
1  while i < a.Length
2    decreases a.Length - i
3    invariant 0 <= i <= a.Length
4    invariant forall k :: 0 <= k < i ==> max >= a[k]
5  {
```

The method FindMax represents an algorithm for finding the maximum element in an array. We will agree that its specifications correspondingly capture the meaning of the algorithm – this very agreement allows us to prove correctness. The thing with specifications is that we can add as many logical formulas as we want, but essentially it is an optimization problem – we need to choose the smallest amount of specifications that properly capture the algorithm we have in mind. In this specific case, the main specification was $\forall k, 0 < k < |a| \rightarrow max \geq [k]$.

CHAPTER 7

Mathematical Induction

Mathematical induction was mentioned earlier briefly when we discussed Peano's axioms. In this chapter, we will provide the exact definition of it.

 Definition 1 **Mathematical induction** is a proof method that is used to prove that a predicate $P(n)$ is true for all natural numbers n. It consists of proving two parts: a base case and an inductive step.

- For the **base** case, we need to show that what we want to prove $P(n)$ is true for some starting value k, which is usually zero – $P(0)$.

- For the **inductive** step, we need to prove that $P(n) \rightarrow P(n + 1)$, that is, if we assume that $P(n)$ is true, then $P(n + 1)$ must follow as a consequence.

After proving the two parts, we can conclude that $P(n)$ holds for all natural numbers. Basically, the formula that we need to prove is $P(0) \wedge (P(n) \rightarrow P(n + 1))$.

© Boro Sitnikovski 2022
B. Sitnikovski, *Introducing Software Verification with Dafny Language*,
https://doi.org/10.1007/978-1-4842-7978-6_7

Mathematical induction is usually defined as an axiom in a formal system. To understand why it works, as an example, it is best to visualize dominoes arranged in a sequence. If we push the first domino, it will push the second, which will push the third, and so on to infinity.

Figure 7-1. *Dominoes*

That is, if we position the dominoes such that if one falls it will push the next one (i.e., $P(n)$ implies $P(n + 1)$) and we push the first one $P(0)$, then all the dominoes will fall (i.e., $P(n)$ is true in general).

To show an example usage of mathematical induction, we consider the following definition.

ⓘ   Definition 2   Consider the following recursive definition for adding numbers:

- Zero is a left identity for addition, that is, $n = 0 + n$.

- $S(m) + n = S(m + n)$, where S is the successor function, that is, $S(0) = 1$, $S(1) = 2$, etc.

Next, in order to prove that $\forall n$, $n + 0 = n$ in the system of Peano's axioms, we can proceed by induction (which is an axiom in this system). For the base case, we have that $0 + 0 = 0$, which is true (by definition of adding numbers, for $n = 0$). For the inductive step, we first assume that $n + 0 = n$ is true (since otherwise the expression is vacuously true) and prove that $S(n) + 0 = S(n)$.

By definition of addition, we have $S(n) + 0 = S(n + 0)$. If we use the inductive hypothesis, we have $S(n) + 0 = S(n)$, which is what we needed to show.

To prove the same in Dafny, we can use the following code:

```
1  predicate P1(n : nat)
2  {
3    n + 0 == n
4  }
5
6  method Example1()
7    ensures forall n :: P1(n)
8  {}
```

However, we didn't have to use induction explicitly here. It is so because Dafny is smart enough to prove this automatically.

7.1. Induction in Dafny

This section will show an example where it is required to explicitly specify that we are using induction within a proof.

Induction and recursion are closely related to each other. We will show this in the next example, in which we will provide two recursive functions, where the first one calculates $\sum_{i=0}^{n} i$ and the second one calculates $\dfrac{n \cdot (n+1)}{2}$, respectively.

```
1  function Sum(n : nat) : nat
2    decreases n
3  {
4    if n == 0 then 0 else n + Sum(n-1)
5  }
6
7  function Sum2(n : nat) : nat
8  {
9    n * (n+1)/2
10 }
```

We can try to prove that these two computations are equivalent for some value of n (they produce the same result), as follows:

```
1  method Main()
2  {
3    assert forall n :: 0 <= n ==> Sum(n) == Sum2(n);
4  }
```

In this case, Dafny will return an error, so we cannot use this to prove the claim and we need to approach the proof differently.

One way we can solve this error is using lemmas and the special syntax {:induction n}, as follows:

```
1  lemma {:induction n} SumLemma(n : nat)
2    ensures Sum(n) == Sum2(n)
3  {}
```

It was only necessary to tell Dafny that we want to use induction on n, and Dafny can automatically prove the claim for us, saving us the manual work. The body is empty because Dafny successfully proves this claim automatically.

Recursion itself represents computation, while induction allows us to prove some property about that computation. As we've seen in Section 3.4, loops can also be represented with nonrecursive methods (imperative style), in contrast to recursive methods. For non-recursive methods, `while` corresponds to recursion (computation), and `invariant` corresponds to induction.

7.2. Manually Proving Induction in Dafny

While invariants are powerful, working with them can be a little tricky. For example, when using them, which invariant property should we add to satisfy Dafny? This is not always obvious. If one knows how to do manual proofs, this might give a better insight into what Dafny is expecting.

Dafny is an automated theorem prover, and some mathematical proofs can be done automatically. But they can also be proven manually, as we show next.

For the sake of example, we will start with the definition of natural numbers; the reason we will use Nat instead of nat is that it will allow for easier pattern matching. Recall their definition, which was mentioned briefly in Section 3.5, together with the addition function that corresponds to Definition 2 of this chapter:

```
1  datatype Nat = Z | S(Nat)
2
3  function Plus(x : Nat, y : Nat) : Nat
4    decreases x;
5  {
6    match x {
7      case Z => y
8      case S(z) => S(Plus(z, y))
9    }
10 }
```

Now, similar to the previous example, we can prove that $n + 0 = n$:

```
1  lemma {:induction n} Example(n : Nat)
2    decreases n;
3    ensures Plus(n, Z) == n
4  {}
```

However, we can also be extra explicit with the proof, and instead of letting Dafny solve it automatically, we show it the way.

```
1  lemma {:induction false} ExampleManual(n : Nat)
2    decreases n;
3    ensures Plus(n, Z) == n
4  {
5    match n {
6      case Z => {
7        // Dafny knows that Plus(Z, Z) == Z
8        // by definition of Plus
9        assert Plus(Z, Z) == Z;
10     }
11     case S(k) => {
12       assert Plus(n, Z) == S(Plus(k, Z));
13       // Hint Dafny that Plus(k, Z) == k
14       ExampleManual(k);
15       assert S(Plus(k, Z)) == S(k);
16       assert S(k) == n;
17     }
18   }
19 }
```

We used pattern matching for proof by cases; recall that lemma is similar to a method, so pattern matching (if-then-else) corresponds to proof by cases. For each case of the induction, we added assertions that start with an expression from the left side of the equality, and in each subsequent step, the final result from the right side of the equality is gradually reached. In addition, with `{:induction false}` we disabled induction since Dafny would've proven it automatically otherwise.

Proofs done in this proof system are very similar to the three-column proofs, as shown in Section 5.2.

Manual proofs like this one are based on so-called structured calculation [11]; more specifically, Dafny uses the following rule of inference:

$$\frac{\Gamma_1 \vdash A = B \quad \Gamma_2 \vdash B = C}{\Gamma_1 \cup \Gamma_2 \vdash A = C}$$

That is, if in some environments (statement lists) it holds that $A = B$ and $B = C$, then from these environments together it can be concluded that $A = C$. To prove a property that $A = B = \ldots = Z$, we repeatedly apply the rule. If any of the formulas do not match the previous one or the one that follows, Dafny will return an error.

For example, for Dafny to be able to complete the proof, we needed to enrich one of these environments with the call to `ExampleManual(k)`.

CHAPTER 8

Verification Exercises

In this chapter, we will provide exercises that can be used to both test your skills and further show what can be proven with Dafny, on the more practical side. For each of the exercises, we will provide its corresponding solution.

8.1. An Odd Implementation

 Exercise 1   Write a predicate OddPred that takes a nat and returns true if the number is odd, and false otherwise. Test your predicate with several cases by creating a lemma TestOddPred. Restriction: do not use recursion or loops.

 Exercise 2   Write a function Odd that takes a nat and returns true if the number is odd, and false otherwise. Use recursion to compute the result. Test your function with several cases by creating a lemma TestOdd.

 Exercise 3   Write a function OddTail that takes a nat and returns true if the number is odd, and false otherwise. Use tail recursion to compute the result. Test your function with several cases by creating a lemma TestOddTail.

© Boro Sitnikovski 2022
B. Sitnikovski, *Introducing Software Verification with Dafny Language*,
https://doi.org/10.1007/978-1-4842-7978-6_8

Exercise 4   Test the following lemmas with your code.

```
1  lemma {:induction n} OddLemma1(n : nat)
2    requires n % 2 == 1
3    ensures OddTail(n, true)
4    ensures Odd(n)
5  {}
6
7  lemma {:induction n} OddLemma2(n : nat)
8    ensures OddPred(n) == Odd(n)
9  {}
```

Exercise 5   Write a predicate OddNat that takes a Nat (the data type that we defined earlier) and returns true if the number is odd, and false otherwise. Use recursion to compute the result. Test your predicate with several cases by creating a lemma TestOddNat.

Exercise 6   Write a method OddMethod that takes a nat and returns true if the number is odd, and false otherwise. Use while loops to compute the result. Test your function by printing the values of a few numbers in the method Main.

8.2. Sunday

 Exercise 7   Prove that there is a Sunday every 7 days by means of a formal proof.

 Exercise 8   Prove that there is a Sunday every 7 days in Dafny. Use the following definitions to map days to numbers to help with your proof using induction.

```
1  datatype Day = Monday | Tuesday | Wednesday | Thursday |
   Friday | Saturday | Sunday
2  datatype Nat = S(Nat) | Z
3
4  function NatToDay(n : Nat) : Day
5    decreases n
6  {
7    match n {
8      case Z                      => Monday
9      case S(Z)                   => Tuesday
10     case S(S(Z))                => Wednesday
11     case S(S(S(Z)))             => Thursday
12     case S(S(S(S(Z))))          => Friday
13     case S(S(S(S(S(Z)))))       => Saturday
14     case S(S(S(S(S(S(Z))))))    => Sunday
15     case S(S(S(S(S(S(S(k)))))))=> NatToDay(k)
16   }
17 }
```

8.3. Mathematical Properties

 Exercise 9   Find a function f such that it satisfies the lemma:

```
1 lemma Idempotence()
2   ensures forall x :: f(f(x)) == f(x)
3 {}
```

 Exercise 10   Find a function f such that it satisfies the lemma:

```
1 lemma Injection()
2   ensures forall x, y :: f(x) == f(y) ==> x == y
3 {}
```

 Exercise 11   Find functions f, g such that they satisfy the lemma:

```
1 lemma CommutativeComposition()
2   ensures forall x :: f(g(x)) == g(f(x))
3  {}
```

8.4. Algebra

 Exercise 12   Provide a recursive function that accepts an Expr and returns a natural number, computing the expression where Add represents addition and Sub represents subtraction for the following data type:

```
1 datatype Expr = Add(Expr, Expr) | Sub(Expr,
  Expr) | N(nat)
```

Definition 1   The binary relation R of a set S is a partial order if the following properties are satisfied:

- $\forall a \in S, aRa$ – reflexivity

- $\forall a, b, c \in S, aRb \wedge bRc \rightarrow aRc$ – transitivity

- $\forall a, b \in S, aRb \wedge bRa \rightarrow a = b$ – antisymmetry

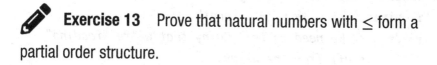 **Exercise 13**   Prove that natural numbers with $\leq$ form a partial order structure.

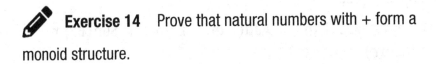

Definition 2   The binary relation R of a set S is a monoid if the following properties are satisfied:

- $\forall a, b, c \in S, (aRb)Rc = aR(bRc)$ – associativity

- $\exists e \forall a, aRe = eRa = a$ – identity

Exercise 14   Prove that natural numbers with + form a monoid structure.

8.5. Miscellaneous Algorithms

Exercise 15   Complete the definition of `CalculateProduct` so that it satisfies the specifications:

```
1  function ProductTo(a : array<nat>, n : nat) : nat
2    requires 0 <= n && n <= a.Length
3    reads a // We need to tell Dafny that we're "reading"
               stuff from the array
4  {
5    if n == 0 then 1 else a[n-1] * ProductTo(a, n-1)
6  }
7  method CalculateProduct(a : array<nat>) returns
   (product : nat)
8    ensures product == ProductTo(a, a.Length)
```

```
 9  {
10    var i := 0;
11    product := 1;
12    while i < a.Length
13      invariant 0 <= i && i <= a.Length
14    {
15    }
16  }
```

 Exercise 16   Implement a function `ProductToSeq` that

works similarly like `ProductTo`, but for `seq<nat>` instead of
`array<nat>`. Further, implement a function `Product` that accepts a
`seq<nat>` and returns a nat which calculates the product of all
numbers in the sequence. Can you implement `Product` but for
arrays instead of sequences? Why or why not?

 Exercise 17   Complete the following method that calculates

the multiplication of numbers using recursion.

```
1  method Multiply(x : int, y : int) returns (r : int)
2    requires 0 <= x && 0 <= y
3    ensures r == x*y
4    decreases x
5  {
6  }
```

✏️ **Exercise 18**   In the following code, a data type is created that allows representing lists; for example, `Cons(1, Cons(2, Nil))` represents the list (1, 2). Complete the implementation of the function `ListMap`. It should accept a function and a list, and apply the function to every element in the list.

```
1  datatype List<T> = Cons(T, List<T>) | Nil
2
3  function method ListMap<T,X>(f : (T -> X), l : List<T>) :
       List<X>
4      ensures ListMap(x => x + 1, Cons(1, Cons(2, Nil))) ==
           Cons(2, Cons(3, Nil))
5  {
6    match l {
7    }
8  }
```

ℹ️ **Definition 3**   Factorial is defined as

$$x! = \begin{cases} 1, & x=0 \\ x \cdot (x-1)! & \text{otherwise} \end{cases}$$

✏️ **Exercise 19**   Find the Hoare triple that expresses the given invariant for factorial and then complete the implementation.

```
1  function Fact(n : nat) : nat
2    decreases n
3  {
4    if n == 0 then 1 else n * Fact(n - 1)
5  }
6
7  method FactMethod(n : nat) returns (f : nat)
8    ensures f == Fact(n)
9  {
10   var i := 0;
11   f := 1;
12   while i < n
13     // We need to tell Dafny that in each iteration,
14     // i <= n is true, so that we can conclude i == n.
15     invariant i <= n
16     invariant f == Fact(i)
17     decreases n - i
18   {
19     i := i + 1;
20     // ?
21   }
22   assert i == n;
23   // From the invariant, Dafny can now deduce that
24   // f == Fact(i). But since i == n, f == Fact(n).
25 }
```

Exercise 20   Given the following code that represents a

robot for the automated delivery of pizzas, do the following:

- Print the commands that the robot needs to execute
  (return value of GetCommands) in order to deliver a
  pizza starting from (0, 0) to (3, 3).

- Prove that the robot always drops a pizza for any
  coordinates when starting at (0, 0).

```
1  datatype Command = Up | Down | Left | Right | Deliver
2  datatype Point<T> = Point(x : T, y : T)
3
4  function method GetCommands(a : Point<nat>, b :
   Point<nat>) :
     seq<Command>
5    decreases a.x, a.y, b.x, b.y
6  {
7    if a.x > b.x then [Left] + GetCommands(Point
     (a.x - 1, a.y),
        Point(b.x, b.y))
8    else if a.y < b.y then [Down] + GetCommands(Point(a.x,
        a.y), Point(b.x, b.y - 1))
9    else if a.y > b.y then [Up] +
     GetCommands(Point(a.x, a.y -
        1), Point(b.x, b.y))
10   else if a.x < b.x then [Right] + GetCommands(Point(a.x,
        a.y), Point(b.x - 1, b.y))
11   else [Deliver]
12 }
```

Exercise 21   Complete the method that calculates the *n*-th Fibonacci number:

```
1   function Fibonacci(n : nat) : nat
2     decreases n
3   {
4     if n <= 1 then n else Fibonacci(n-2) + Fibonacci(n-1)
5   }
6
7   method Fib(n: nat) returns (f1 : nat)
8     ensures f1 == Fibonacci(n)
9   {
10    var i := 0;
11    f1 := 0;
12    var f2 := 1;
13    var tmp : nat;
14    while i < n
15    decreases n - i
16      invariant 0 <= i <= n
17      invariant i == 0 ==> f2 == 1
18      invariant i > 0 ==> f2 == Fibonacci(i - 1)
19      invariant f1 == Fibonacci(i)
20    {
21    }
22  }
```

Exercise 22   The following code uses the `Tree` data type from Section 3.5. It also provides a function for calculating all possible paths for a given tree. Study the implementation, and then construct a few trees and print their paths.

```
1   datatype Tree<T> = Leaf | Node(T, Tree, Tree)
2
3   function method GetTreePaths(tree : Tree<nat>, acc :
        seq<nat>) : set<seq<nat>>
4     decreases tree, acc
5   {
6     match tree {
7       case Leaf => if |acc| > 0 then {acc} else {}
8       case Node(x, Leaf, r) => GetTreePaths(r, acc + [x])
9       case Node(x, l, Leaf) => GetTreePaths(l, acc + [x])
10      case Node(x, l, r) => GetTreePaths(l, acc + [x]) +
              GetTreePaths(r, acc + [x])
11    }
12  }
13
14  method Main()
15  {
16  }
```

8.6. Prime Numbers

 Exercise 23   Fix the following code by introducing a bound argument to the function:

```
1  predicate IsPrime(n : nat)
2  {
3    2 <= n && forall m :: 2 <= m < n ==> n % m != 0
4  }
5
6  function GetPrimeAfter(n : nat) : nat
7  {
8    if IsPrime(n + 1) then n + 1
9    else GetPrimeAfter(n + 1)
10 }
```

 Exercise 24   In Exercise 20, you chose to return some default value in case the bound was reached. Use the following data type and return Nothing if the bound was reached, and otherwise, use Just on the value.

```
1  datatype Maybe<T> = Just(T) | Nothing
```

 Exercise 25   Implement a new predicate, IsPrime2, which is similar to the predicate IsPrime and which uses the Factors helper function. Make sure it passes the TestPrimes lemma.

```
1  function FactorsTail(n : nat, m : nat) : seq<nat>
2    decreases m
3  {
4    if m == 0 then []
5    else if n % m == 0 then [m] + FactorsTail(n, m - 1)
6    else FactorsTail(n, m - 1)
7  }
8
9  function Factors(n : nat) : seq<nat>
10 {
11   FactorsTail(n, n)
12 }
13
14 lemma TestPrimes()
15   ensures IsPrime2(0) <==> IsPrime(0)
16   ensures IsPrime2(1) <==> IsPrime(1)
17   ensures IsPrime2(2) <==> IsPrime(2)
18   ensures IsPrime2(3) <==> IsPrime(3)
19   ensures IsPrime2(4) <==> IsPrime(4)
20 {}
```

8.7. Formal Proofs

 Exercise 26   Complete the following proof that states that there's a unique element 1:

```
1  predicate P(x : nat) {
2    x == 1
3  }
4
```

```
5  method EgUniqueness()
6    ensures exists x :: P(x) && forall x, y :: P(x) && P(y) ==>
         x == y
7  {
8  }
```

✐ Exercise 27   Complete the following proof:

```
1  method EgCases()
2    ensures 1 + 1 == 2 || 2 + 2 == 5
3  {
4    // Suppose 2 + 2 == 5
5    if ... {
6      // In this case, 1 + 1 != 2
7      assert ...;
8      // Which is clearly false
9      assert false;
10   }
11   // Suppose 1 + 1 == 2
12   if ... {
13     // This is clearly true
14     assert true;
15   }
16   // Since at least one case was true:
17   assert 1 + 1 == 2 || 2 + 2 == 5;
18 }
```

Exercise 28   Fix the following broken proof:

```
1  method EgImpl(p : bool, q : bool)
2    ensures (p && (p ==> q)) ==> q
3  {
4    if p {
5      if q ==> p {
6          assert q;
7      }
8    }
9  }
```

 Exercise 29   Write a proof that states the modus ponens rule (Exercise 25), but at the meta-level instead of the object level (using requires and ensures).

8.8. Solutions

Exercise 1

```
1  predicate OddPred(n : nat)
2  {
3    n % 2 == 1
4  }
5  lemma TestOddPred()
6    ensures !OddPred(0)
7    ensures OddPred(1)
8    ensures !OddPred(2)
9    ensures OddPred(3)
10 {}
```

Exercise 2

```
1  function Odd(n : nat) : bool
2    decreases n
3  {
4    if n == 1 then true
5    else if n == 0 then false
6    else !Odd(n - 1)
7  }
8  lemma TestOdd()
9    ensures !Odd(0)
10   ensures Odd(1)
11   ensures !Odd(2)
12   ensures Odd(3)
13 {}
```

Exercise 3

```
1  function OddTail (n : nat, o : bool) : bool
2    decreases n
3  {
4    if n == 1 then o
5    else if n == 0 then !o
6    else OddTail(n - 1, !o)
7  }
8
9  lemma TestOddTail()
10   ensures !OddTail(0, true)
11   ensures OddTail(1, true)
12   ensures !OddTail(2, true)
13   ensures OddTail(3, true)
14   ensures !OddTail(4, true)
15 {}
```

Exercise 5

```
1   datatype Nat = Z | S(Nat)
2
3   predicate OddNat(n : Nat)
4     decreases n
5   {
6     match n {
7       case Z => false
8       case S(Z) => true
9       case S(x) => !OddNat(x)
10   }
11   }
12
13  lemma TestOddNat()
14    ensures !OddNat(Z)
15    ensures OddNat(S(Z))
16    ensures !OddNat(S(S(Z)))
17    ensures OddNat(S(S(S(Z))))
18    ensures !OddNat(S(S(S(S(Z)))))
19  {}
```

Exercise 6

```
1   method OddMethod(n : nat) returns (odd : bool)
2   {
3     var x := n;
4     while x > 2
5       decreases x - 2
6     {
7       x := x - 2;
8     }
9     odd := x != 1;
```

```
10  }
11
12  method Main()
13  {
14    var x := OddMethod(0);
15    print(x);
16    x := OddMethod(1);
17    print(x);
18    x := OddMethod(2);
19    print(x);
20    x := OddMethod(3);
21    print(x);
22  }
```

Exercise 7

We will prove that there is one Sunday in the range $(N, N + 6)$. For this, we can use proof by cases where each case will be a day of the week. Thus, the day N is one of

- Sunday: Thus, N is Sunday.

- Saturday: Thus, $N + 1$ is Sunday.

- Friday: Thus, $N + 2$ is Sunday.

- Thursday: Thus, $N + 3$ is Sunday.

- Wednesday: Thus, $N + 4$ is Sunday.

- Tuesday: Thus, $N + 5$ is Sunday.

- Monday: Thus, $N + 6$ is Sunday.

In any case, for any N, there is one Sunday in the range $(N, N + 6)$. That is, there is one Sunday every $N + 6 - N + 1 = 7$ days.

Exercise 8

```
1  lemma {:induction n} proof(n : Nat)
2    ensures NatToDay(n) == Sunday ==> NatToDay(n) == Sunday
3    ensures NatToDay(n) == Saturday ==> NatToDay(S(n)) ==
         Sunday
4    ensures NatToDay(n) == Friday ==> NatToDay(S(S(n))) ==
         Sunday
5    ensures NatToDay(n) == Thursday ==> NatToDay(S(S(S(n))))
         == Sunday
6    ensures NatToDay(n) == Wednesday ==>
         NatToDay(S(S(S(S(n))))) == Sunday
7    ensures NatToDay(n) == Tuesday ==>
         NatToDay(S(S(S(S(S(n)))))) == Sunday
8    ensures NatToDay(n) == Monday ==>
         NatToDay(S(S(S(S(S(S(n))))))) == Sunday
9  {}
```

Exercise 9

```
1  function f(x : nat) : nat
2  {
3    x
4  }
```

The functions $f(x) = x \cdot 0$, $f(x) = x \cdot 1$, $f(x) = x + 0$ also work. Basically, any function that has no additional effect if it is called multiple times with the same arguments.

Exercise 10

Again,

```
1  function f(x : nat) : nat
2  {
3    x
4  }
```

Also, some other functions are $f(x) = x + 2$, $f(x) = x \cdot 5$. But this one isn't: $f(x) = 0$. Can you think why?

Exercise 11

Similarly to before, we can use $f(x) = x$ and $g(x) = x$.

Exercise 12

```
1  function ComputeExpr (e : Expr) : nat
2  {
3    match e {
4      case N(x) => x
5      case Add(x, y) => ComputeExpr(x) + ComputeExpr(y)
6      case Sub(x, y) => ComputeExpr(x) - ComputeExpr(y)
7    }
8  }
```

Exercise 13

```
1  predicate Order(a : nat, b : nat)
2  {
3    a <= b
4  }
5  lemma Reflexive()
6    ensures forall a :: Order(a, a)
7  {}
```

```
 8  lemma Transitive()
 9    ensures forall a, b, c :: Order(a, b) && Order(b, c) ==>
        Order(a, c)
10  {}
11  lemma Total()
12    ensures forall a, b :: Order(a, b) && Order(b, a)
      ==> a == b
13  {}
```

Exercise 14

```
 1  function Plus(a : nat, b : nat) : nat
 2  {
 3    a + b
 4  }
 5  lemma Associativity()
 6    ensures forall a, b, c :: Plus(Plus(a, b), c) == Plus(a,
        Plus(b, c))
 7  {}
 8  lemma Identity(a : nat)
 9    ensures exists e :: Plus(a, e) == Plus(e, a) && Plus(e, a)
        == a
10  {
11    match a {
12      case 0 =>
13        assert Plus(0, 0) == 0;
14      case n =>
15        assert Plus(n, 0) == n;
16    }
17  }
```

```
18  lemma Monoid()
19  {
20    Associativity();
21    Identity(0);
22  }
```

Exercise 15

```
1     decreases a.Length - i
2     invariant product == ProductTo(a, i)
3   {
4     product := product * a[i];
5     i := i + 1;
6   }
```

Exercise 16

```
1   function ProductToSeq (a : seq<nat>, n : nat) : nat
2     requires 0 <= n && n <= |a|
3     decreases a, n
4   {
5     if n == 0 then 1 else a[n-1] * ProductToSeq(a, n-1)
6   }
7
8   function Product(a : seq<nat>) : nat
9     decreases a
10  {
11    if |a| == 0 then 1 else a[0] * Product(a[1..])
12  }
```

The reason we can't do the same implementation using arrays is that they don't have built-in support for calculating a subarray.

Exercise 17

```
1  {
2    if x == 0 {
3       r := 0;
4    } else {
5       var m := multiply(x-1, y);
6       r := m + x;
7    }
8  }
```

Exercise 18

```
1  function method ListMap<T,X>(f : (T -> X), l : List<T>) :
     List<X>
2    ensures ListMap(x => x + 1, Cons(1, Cons(2, Nil))) ==
     Cons(2, Cons(3, Nil))
3  {
4    match l {
5      case Nil => Nil
6      case Cons(n, l') => Cons(f(n), ListMap(f, l'))
7    }
8  }
```

Exercise 19

We are looking for the following Hoare triple:

$$\{f = i!\}i := i + 1; ?; \{f = (i + 1)!\}$$

The only way we can get from $f = i!$ to $f = (i + 1)!$ is if we multiply f by $i + 1$; this would make $f \cdot (i + 1) = i! \cdot (i + 1) = (i + 1)!$, per definition of factorial. But since i is already incremented before the command ?, we only need to multiply f by i.

$$\{f = i!\}i := i + 1; f := f \cdot i; \{f = (i + 1)!\}$$

The command is f := f * i.

Exercise 20

```
1  method Main()
2  {
3    var delivery_path := GetCommands(Point(0, 0),
     Point(3, 3));
4    print(delivery_path);
5  }
6  lemma {:induction x, y} Proof(x : nat, y : nat)
7    ensures Deliver in GetCommands(Point(0, 0), Point(x, y))
8  {}
```

Exercise 21

```
1    tmp := f1 + f2;
2    f2 := f1;
3    f1 := tmp;
4    i := i + 1;
```

Exercise 22

```
1  method Main()
2  {
3    var t1 := GetTreePaths(Node(1, Leaf, Leaf), []);
4    print(t1);
5    var t2 := GetTreePaths(Node(1, Node(2, Leaf, Leaf), Node(2,
       Leaf, Leaf)), []);
6    print(t2);
7    var t3 := GetTreePaths(Node(1, Node(2, Node(3, Node(4,
       Leaf, Leaf), Leaf), Leaf), Node(3, Leaf, Node(5, Leaf,
       Leaf))), []);
8    print(t3);
9  }
```

Exercise 23

```
1  function GetPrimeAfter(n : nat, bound : nat) : nat
2    decreases bound - n
3  {
4    if n >= bound then 2
5    else if IsPrime(n + 1) then n + 1
6    else GetPrimeAfter(n + 1, bound)
7  }
```

Exercise 24

```
1  function GetPrimeAfter(n : nat, bound : nat) : Maybe<nat>
2    decreases bound - n
3  {
4    if n >= bound then Nothing
5    else if IsPrime(n + 1) then Just(n + 1)
6    else GetPrimeAfter(n + 1, bound)
7  }
```

Exercise 25

```
1  predicate IsPrime2(n : nat)
2  {
3    |Factors(n)| == 2
4  }
```

Exercise 26

```
1  method EgUniqueness ()
2    ensures exists x :: P(x) && forall x, y :: P(x) && P(y) ==>
       x == y
3  {
4    assert P(1);
5  }
```

Exercise 27

```
1   method EgCases()
2     ensures 1 + 1 == 2 || 2 + 2 == 5
3   {
4     // Suppose 2 + 2 == 5
5     if 2 + 2 == 5 {
6       // In this case, 1 + 1 != 2
7       assert 1 + 1 != 2;
8       // Which is clearly false
9       assert false;
10    }
11    // Suppose 1 + 1 == 2
12    if 1 + 1 == 2 {
13      // This is clearly true
14      assert true;
15    }
16    // Since at least one case was true:
17    assert 1 + 1 == 2 || 2 + 2 == 5;
18  }
```

Exercise 28

```
1   method EgImpl(p : bool, q : bool)
2     ensures (p && (p ==> q)) ==> q
3   {
4     if p {
5       if p ==> q {
6         assert q;
7       }
8     }
9   }
```

Exercise 29

```
1  method EgImpl2(p : bool, q : bool)
2    requires p
3    requires p ==> q
4    ensures q
5  {
6    assert p;
7    assert p ==> q;
8    assert q;
9  }
```

CHAPTER 9

Implementing a Formal System

So far, we have been mostly using a set of formal systems to prove software correctness. In this final chapter, we show how to *both* create and use a formal system in order to be able to prove facts. For that, we will provide a minimal implementation[1] of propositional logic, as described in Chapter 2. For a more advanced implementation of a formal system, see [7].

The syntax of the formal system expressed in BNF (Backus-Naur form) is

```
1  prop ::= P | Q | R | unop prop | prop brelop prop
2  unop ::= "!"
3  brelop ::= "&&" | "||" | "->"
```

The code in Dafny, which follows the same syntax:

```
1  datatype Prop =
2    P | Q | R
3    | Not (Prop)
4    | And (Prop, Prop)
5    | Or (Prop, Prop)
6    | Imp (Prop, Prop)
```

---

[1] Recursion is sufficient to represent a complex formal system. However, the system that we'll build is basic; it won't rely on recursion at all.

© Boro Sitnikovski 2022
B. Sitnikovski, *Introducing Software Verification with Dafny Language*,
https://doi.org/10.1007/978-1-4842-7978-6_9

We now have a way to represent some logical formulas, for example, $P \wedge Q$ as And(P, Q). In Dafny, we get construction of well-formed formulas for free due to algebraic data structures. In some untyped programming languages, such as Python, we could use hashmaps to simulate the types.

```python
# Python
def And(x, y):
    return {'x': x, 'y': y, 'type': 'and'}

def Imp(x, y):
    return {'x': x, 'y': y, 'type': 'imp'}
```

Further, in our implementation, we also need a way to differentiate between well-formed formulas and theorems since not all well-formed formulas are theorems. For that, we provide the Proof data type and a way to extract a proof:

```
//datatype Prop = ...
datatype Proof<T> = Proof(T)
function method FromProof(x : Proof<Prop>) : Prop
{
  match x {
    case Proof(a) => a
  }
}
```

Note that Proof(And(P, Q)) ($\vdash P \wedge Q$) is different from And(P, Q) ($P \wedge Q$). Here's how we can construct and destruct (extract) proofs in Python:

```python
# Python
def Proof(x):
    return {'v': x, 'type': 'proof'}
def FromProof(x):
    if not isinstance(x, dict) or not 'v' in x: return None
    return x['v']
```

Note in the Python code how we have to be extra careful with the conditional checks, whereas in Dafny, it is much simpler due to pattern matching.

The Proof constructor mustn't be used directly; proofs should only be constructed given the rules that we provide next.

```
1  function method RuleJoin(x : Proof<Prop>, y : Proof<Prop>) :
       Proof<Prop>
2  {
3    Proof(And(FromProof(x), FromProof(y)))
4  }
5  function method RuleSepL(x : Proof<Prop>) : Proof<Prop>
6  {
7    match FromProof(x) {
8      case And(a, b) => Proof(a)
9      case x => Proof(x)
10   }
11 }
```

The preceding implementation corresponds to the following rules:

$$\frac{A \quad B}{A \wedge B}(\textbf{RuleJoin}) \quad \frac{A \wedge B}{A}(\textbf{RuleSepL})$$

These rules come from GEB [1], and we list all of them here for completeness:

- Joining Rule (And-introduction): If x and y are theorems, then $x \wedge y$ is a theorem.

- Sep Rule (And-elimination): If $x \wedge y$ is a theorem, then both x and y are theorems.

- Fantasy Rule (Implication-introduction): If x were a theorem, y would be a theorem $(x \rightarrow y)$.

- Contrapositive Rule: $x \to y$ and $\neg y \to \neg x$ are interchangeable.

- De Morgan's Rule: $\neg x \wedge \neg y$ and $\neg(x \vee y)$ are interchangeable.

- Double-Tilde Rule (Double negation): The string $\neg\neg$ can be deleted from any theorem. It can also be inserted into any theorem.

- Rule of Detachment (Implication-elimination): If x and $x \to y$ are both theorems, then y is a theorem.

- Switcheroo Rule: $x \vee y$ and $\neg x \to y$ are interchangeable.

The most powerful rule is the **Fantasy Rule**, implemented as follows:

```
1  function method RuleFantasy(x : Prop, y : (Proof<Prop> ->
       Proof<Prop>)) : Proof<Prop>
2  {
3    Proof(Imp(x, FromProof(y(Proof(x)))))
4  }
```

RuleFantasy accepts a non-proven term x : Prop, whereas other rules accept proven terms; the hypothesis needn't be necessarily true, it only states that "If this hypothesis were a theorem, then that would be a theorem." The second argument is a function y : (Proof<Prop> -> Proof<Prop>) that accepts a Proof and returns a Proof, basically another rule that will be used to transform the hypothesis x. As a result, it produces the theorem $x \to y(x)$.

Here's the same implementation of the previous rules in Python:

```
1  # Python
2  def RuleJoin(x, y):
3      if not isinstance(x, dict) or not isinstance(y, dict) or
           not 'type' in x or not 'type' in y or x['type'] !=
           'proof' or y['type'] != 'proof': return None
```

```
4      return Proof(And(FromProof(x), FromProof(y)))
5   def RuleSepL(x):
6      if not isinstance(x, dict) or not 'type' in x or x['type']
           != 'proof': return None
7      wff = FromProof(x)
8      if wff['type'] == 'and': return Proof(wff['x'])
9      return Proof(wff)
10  def RuleFantasy(x, y):
11     if not isinstance(x, dict) or not 'type' in x or not
           callable(y): return None
12     return Proof(Imp(x, FromProof(y(Proof(x)))))
```

For most rules, we can write intro (RuleJoin) and elim (RuleSepL) functions. Here's another example of a rule that performs interchanging of formulas:

```
1   function method RuleDeMorgan(x : Proof<Prop>) : Proof<Prop>
2   {
3     match FromProof(x) {
4       case And(Not(a), Not(b)) => Proof(Not(Or(a, b)))
5       case Not(Or(a, b)) => Proof(And(Not(a), Not(b)))
6       case x => Proof(x)
7     }
8   }
```

Since we defined the rules in Dafny as function method, we can build proofs iteratively by printing the results. For example, we can prove that $\vdash P \wedge Q \to P \wedge P$ as follows:

```
1   method Main()
2   {
3     var p_and_q := And(P, Q);
4     var join := (x) => RuleJoin(RuleSepL(x), RuleSepL(x));
```

```
5    var x := RuleFantasy(p_and_q, join);
6    print(x);
7    assert x == Proof(Imp(p_and_q, And(P, P)));
8  }
9  // Or simply
10  method Example()
11    ensures RuleFantasy(And(P, Q), (x) =>
      RuleJoin(RuleSepL(x),
          RuleSepL(x))) == Proof(Imp(And(P, Q), And(P, P)))
12  {}
```

Note how we embedded a formal system (propositional logic) within a formal system (Dafny/Python), and we were able to reason about it through symbolic manipulation; in Dafny, this corresponds to pattern matching and data types, whereas in Python, it corresponds to conditionals and hashmaps.

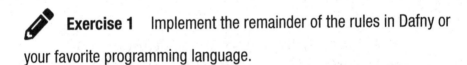 **Exercise 1**   Implement the remainder of the rules in Dafny or your favorite programming language.

Exercise 2   Using the rules you implemented in the previous exercise, prove the following fact in the system: $\neg\neg(\neg P \to Q) \to P \lor Q$.

APPENDIX A

Gödel's Theorems

Hilbert's program was formulated by the mathematician David Hilbert in the early twentieth century. The main goal of this program was to establish the foundations for all mathematics, that is, to define all of mathematics in a single formal system. In other words, the program sought to find a formal system from which one could deduce *all* possible truths about mathematics. In this appendix, we will show the mathematical answer that was found to address this program.

 Definition 1 **Gödel numbering** is a function that assigns a natural number to each symbol or well-formed formula in a formal system.

Table A-1. *Example of Gödel numbering*

Symbol	Number
0	1
1	2
S	3
=	4
+	...
...	...

© Boro Sitnikovski 2022
B. Sitnikovski, *Introducing Software Verification with Dafny Language,*
https://doi.org/10.1007/978-1-4842-7978-6

For example, within Peano's axioms, using Definition 1, we can express self-referential expressions at the object level. With this, the system gains additional power of expressiveness; that is, in a way, the formal system becomes "aware" of itself by being able to refer to its own symbols and formulas.

Considering Table A-1 (where S is the successor function), the following holds, which is a formula about the system within the system itself:[1]

$$1 = S(0) \equiv (2, 4, 3, 1) \equiv (S(S(0)), S(S(S(S(0)))), S(S(S(0))), S(0))$$

As mentioned, the system gains more power of expressiveness, but it is this power that causes the theorems of incompleteness. Let's now consider the following two statements:

1. Snow is white.

2. Snow has four letters.

The first statement is correct, while the second is incorrect. Snow as such does not have four letters (in fact, it does not have a single letter), but "Snow" has four letters. This difference regarding quotation is significant in the proof of Gödel's theorems of incompleteness.

 Definition 2   For an expression P in which the variable x appears, its **diagonalization $D(P(x))$** is the replacement of the variable x with the whole expression in quotation marks.

---

[1] Tuples were used, but although not defined in Peano, they can be encoded in other ways. For example, $(2, 4, 3, 1)$ can be represented by the number $2^2 \cdot 3^4 \cdot 5^3 \cdot 7^1 = 283500$. There exists an algorithm that can extract prime factors from a given number and thus go from 283500 to $(2, 4, 3, 1)$.

For example, for the expression $P(x)$ = Boro is reading x, the diagonalization would be $D(P(x))$ = Boro is reading "Boro is reading x". This allows expressing self-referential statements; consider the following statements:

1. $P(x)$ - Boro is reading the diagonalization of x

2. $Q(x)$ - Boro is reading the diagonalization of "Boro is reading the diagonalization of x"

The second statement expresses that Boro is reading the diagonalization of the first statement, that is, $Q(x)= D(P(x))$. But the diagonalization of the first statement is the second statement, that is, $D(P(x)) = Q(x)$. In fact, the second statement refers to itself.

 Definition 3   A formal system F is

- **Incomplete** if there are statements that are true but which cannot be proved to be true in F

- **Complete** if all true statements in F can be proved

- **Inconsistent** if there is a theorem in F that is contradictory

- **Consistent** if there are no contradictory theorems in F

With Gödel numbering, the statement "this statement is not provable in F" can be represented in the system F itself, where the word "this" can be represented using the concept of diagonalization by pointing to the same statement. Hence, the given statement can be either true or false. In case it is true, then it is not provable in F, so this truth cannot be proved in F. Alternatively, if it is false, then it is provable in F, but something that is false cannot be proved. Thus, *the system is incomplete* because some truths are unprovable in it.

Definition 4   A formal system F contains some statements that cannot be proved in F.

Again, Gödel's numbering can represent the statement "this statement is false in F", where diagonalization can represent the word "this" by pointing to the same statement. The given statement is true if it is false, and therefore, it is neither true nor false. ***The system is inconsistent.***

 Definition 5   A formal system F cannot prove itself to be consistent in F.

It follows that there is no formal system[2] that is both complete and consistent. That is, no system can contain all possible truths, because a given system cannot prove some truths about its own structure. Kurt Gödel proves this with Gödel's theorems of incompleteness and thus answers Hilbert's program.

In general, the focus is often on which parts of mathematics can be formalized into specific formal systems, rather than looking for a theory in which all of mathematics can be formalized. A historical overview of the formalization and truthfulness of mathematics is given in [1, 6] where it is noted that "patterns of reasoning cannot be defended forever, at some point faith takes over." Yet, although imperfect, mathematical systems are still useful tools.

---

[2] Gödel's theorems affect only those systems that allow the expression of arithmetic of natural numbers; the reason for this prerequisite is that the theorems themselves depend on Gödel numbering, which depends on the arithmetic of natural numbers. More specifically, Gödel's theorems affect those systems in which all primitive recursive functions are representable.

Conclusion

In this book, we introduced the mathematical apparatuses and models that allow us to prove the correctness of software. We also introduced Dafny as an example tool that enables software verification. We learned about mathematical logic, how to represent computation, proofs, specifications (preconditions, postconditions, invariants), and how to build a formal system.

We worked through a bunch of exercises, and we managed to prove some properties about specific algorithms. It is useful to know these concepts and how to use them. Even though you may not be using them daily, the very skill gained by learning them will improve your critical thinking. Invariants, preconditions, and postconditions are useful tools, for example, when using a debugger to resolve a bug in a program. Reasoning in terms of invariants and double-checking assumptions is one of the most important characteristics of a programmer.

Besides verifying basic algorithms, there is also a way to add I/O on top of the verified methods by exporting these methods to a standard programming language, such as C# – this would make an application more practical. Dafny already has support for exporting code, and we encourage the reader to research this further.

© Boro Sitnikovski 2022
B. Sitnikovski, *Introducing Software Verification with Dafny Language*,
https://doi.org/10.1007/978-1-4842-7978-6

CONCLUSION

One challenge that arises with verification is to accurately define formal software specifications. What specifications should we choose so that we can say with confidence that our software is correct? What does it mean for our software to be correct in the first place? In addition, since most software development today is done iteratively and quickly, this is not always easy as providing specifications is a time-consuming task.

One final observation to make is the connection with mathematics and that almost everything had to do with the simplification of mathematical expressions through the use of formal systems.

Bibliography

[1] *Hofstadter, Douglas R.* Gödel, Escher, Bach: an eternal golden braid. *Vol. 13. New York: Basic books, 1979.*

[2] *Velleman, Daniel J.* How to prove it: A structured approach. *Cambridge University Press, 2019.*

[3] *Hoare, Charles Antony Richard. "An axiomatic basis for computer programming."* Communications of the ACM *12, no. 10, 1969.*

[4] *Leino, K. Rustan M. "Dafny: An automatic program verifier for functional correctness." In* International Conference on Logic for Programming Artificial Intelligence and Reasoning, *pp. 348–370. Springer, Berlin, Heidelberg, 2010.*

[5] *De Moura, Leonardo, and Nikolaj Bjørner. "Z3-a Tutorial."* Microsoft, Albuquerque, NM, USA, Tech. Rep *2012.*

[6] *Nelson, Edward. "Mathematics and Faith."* URL: `http://math.princeton.edu/~nelson/papers.html, 2002.`

[7] *Sitnikovski, Boro. "Tutorial implementation of Hoare logic in Haskell"* arXiv preprint arXiv:2101.11320, *2021.*

© Boro Sitnikovski 2022
B. Sitnikovski, *Introducing Software Verification with Dafny Language,*
https://doi.org/10.1007/978-1-4842-7978-6

[8]   *Herbert, Luke, K. Rustan M. Leino, and Jose Quaresma. "Using Dafny, an automatic program verifier." In* LASER Summer School on Software Engineering, *pp. 156–181. Springer, Berlin, Heidelberg, 2011.*

[9]   *Halmos, Paul.* Naive Set Theory. *Courier Dover Publications, 1960.*

[10] *Smullyan, Raymond M.* The Gödelian Puzzle Book: Puzzles, Paradoxes and Proofs. *Courier Corporation, 2013.*

[11] *Back, Ralph, Jim Grundy, and Joakim Von Wright. "Structured calculational proof."* Formal Aspects of Computing 9, *no. 5–6, 1997.*

[12] *Pierce, Benjamin C., Arthur Azevedo de Amorim, Chris Casinghino, Marco Gaboardi, Michael Greenberg, Catalin Hriţcu, Vilhelm Sjöberg, and Brent Yorgey. "Logical foundations."* Electronic textbook *2018.*

[13] *McCarthy, John. "Recursive functions of symbolic expressions and their computation by machine, Part I."* Communications of the ACM 3, *no. 4, 1960.*

[14] *Sitnikovski, Boro.* Gentle Introduction to Dependent Types with Idris. *Leanpub/Amazon KDP, 2018.*

Index

A

Algebra, 89, 90
Algebraic data types, 45, 46
Algorithm, 19
Arrays, 70, 71
Assertions, 20
Assignment rule,
      Hoare logic, 63

B

Backus-Naur form, 31
Binary tree, 31
Bounded loops, 29
Bound variable, 47

C

CalculateProduct, 90, 91, 107
Cartesian product, 40
Computation
  algorithm, 19
  functions, 22
  loops, 26
    bounded and
      unbounded, 29
    power and power
      tail, 27–29

methods, 21
  conditionals, 22
  mathematical definition, 23
  multiple returns, 24
  vs. functions, 22
  predicates and lemmas, 25, 26
  variables and assertions, 20, 21
Constraint programming, 65
Contrapositive rule, 116

D

Dafny, 1
  as an automated theorem
    prover, 1
  error at compile time, 5
  extension, 2
  first program, 4
  formal systems, 5
  installation, 2
  Main method, 4
  shares features and concepts
    with languages, 1
  specifications (*see also*
    Specifications)
  VS Code, 1
De Morgan's rule, 116
Double-tilde rule, 116

Printed in the United States
by Baker & Taylor Publisher Services